SURVIVING THE COLLEGE
APPLICATION PROCESS

You have to be angular to fit into a well-rounded college. Colleges seek to be well-rounded so they can offer varied experiences to their students. Students who express their intimate relationship with themselves are more successful in communicating their uniqueness to the college. By providing a variety of case studies Lisa Bleich shows how it's done. Kudos to this author.

—**C. Claire Law**, MS, Certified Educational Planner, co-author of *Find the Perfect College for You*

"In this book, Lisa Bleich effectively marries her extensive knowledge of marketing with her experience as an independent college consultant and mentor. Her advice to students is critical in the current admission environment: identify and communicate your unique and authentic strengths, talents and experiences to make you an angular, and therefore more compelling, candidate. By applying the principles of marketing she helps students understand how to represent the best of who they are to the admissions office."

—**Mark H. Sklarow**, Chief Executive Officer, Independent Educational Consultants Association

"Bleich takes the guesswork out of the college application process. Her case studies are easily adapted to fit any student's college planning needs. *Surviving the College Application Process* is informative, easy to read, and fun."

—**Steven R. Antonoff**, Ph.D., CEP, author of *The College Finder: Choose the School That's Right for You!*

SURVIVING
THE COLLEGE
APPLICATION
PROCESS

CASE STUDIES TO HELP YOU FIND
YOUR UNIQUE ANGLE FOR SUCCESS

Lisa Bleich

NEW YORK

SURVIVING THE COLLEGE **APPLICATION** PROCESS
CASE STUDIES TO HELP YOU FIND YOUR UNIQUE ANGLE FOR SUCCESS

© 2014 **Lisa Bleich**.

Published in New York, New York, by Morgan James Publishing. Morgan James and The Entrepreneurial Publisher are trademarks of Morgan James, LLC. www.MorganJamesPublishing.com

The Morgan James Speakers Group can bring authors to your live event. For more information or to book an event visit The Morgan James Speakers Group at www.TheMorganJamesSpeakersGroup.com.

Note: Student names have been changed for privacy.

FREE eBook edition for your existing eReader with purchase

PRINT NAME ABOVE

For more information, instructions, restrictions, and to register your copy, go to **www.bitlit.ca/readers/register** or use your QR Reader to scan the barcode:

ISBN 978-1-61448-722-7 paperback
ISBN 978-1-61448-723-4 eBook
ISBN 978-1-61448-724-1 audio
ISBN 978-1-61448-884-2 hardcover
Library of Congress Control Number:
2013946288

Cover Design by:
Rachel Lopez
www.r2cdesign.com

Interior Design by:
Bonnie Bushman
bonnie@caboodlegraphics.com

In an effort to support local communities, raise awareness and funds, Morgan James Publishing donates a percentage of all book sales for the life of each book to Habitat for Humanity Peninsula and Greater Williamsburg.

Get involved today, visit
www.MorganJamesBuilds.com

Habitat
for Humanity®
Peninsula and
Greater Williamsburg
Building Partner

CONTENTS

A NOTE TO PARENTS:
WHY I CAN HELP YOUR KID GET INTO COLLEGE

When I moved to New Jersey from California in 2004, one of the first things I noticed was how stressed out most parents were about the college application process. They understood that a college education was a prerequisite to getting ahead, but as the application pool was becoming increasingly crowded and competitive, they weren't sure how to help their kids stand out to admissions committees while competing with thousands of other kids for relatively few freshmen slots. Not only that, the application process had changed since they applied to college; now, it was a lot more multilayered and, well, daunting.

I could certainly sympathize, but my own kids were still in elementary school at the time, and college seemed a long way off. Nonetheless, the problem interested me. I couldn't help thinking that my previous experience in marketing (as a visiting assistant professor of marketing at Whittier College, director of recruiting for Ticketmaster Online/CitySearch, and a developer of strategic marketing plans for various companies) might lend some much-needed perspective to the challenge these parents and their teens faced. In fact, by using a strategic marketing approach when "positioning" students for college admissions committees, I thought I could help them find a good fit between their needs and what colleges desired from successful applicants. In other words, since I had learned how to position products and services to appeal to customers, I figured I could also position students to be appealing to colleges.

To test my theory, I offered to work pro bono with my next-door neighbor, a high school senior applying to college. Isabelle was a strong student but uncertain about which school would be a good fit for her. She was denied at her top choice, Bowdoin, a small liberal arts college in Maine, but she was accepted to several other small liberal arts colleges along the East Coast, as well as McGill University in Montreal, Canada. Something in Isabelle's gut directed her toward McGill, a large, internationally diverse institution, but she still felt confused and very stressed about making the right decision.

Since Isabelle was my first client, we took a haphazard approach to analyzing the colleges at which she'd been accepted. Ultimately, Isabelle followed her instinct and chose McGill. Thankfully, it was the right decision. Isabelle graduated four years later and is now happily employed in New York City.

While helping my neighbor find the right college, I realized that there had to be a more strategic way to approach this process. So, over the course of the next eight years, I developed a system to help students apply to college. This led to the founding of my company, College Bound Mentor, LLC. My strategic system now includes tools to help students think about who they really are, how they learn best, the types of people around whom they most want to be, the sort of academic social life where they will best thrive, and, most important, what makes them different and unique. In fact, I realized that just as a product or service can be differentiated from other products or services with its unique selling proposition (USP)— something that no other product or service offers—each student also has a unique selling proposition: one that will make him or her attractive to the right school. I also discovered, during hundreds of individual consultations, that every student has innate talents, but the ability to identify those talents and communicate them effectively to colleges is the key to a successful application process. Unfortunately, most kids have a difficult time identifying what parts of their background and experiences are most important and interesting.

Finally, I wanted to make insights like the one I just mentioned, as well as all the tools I had developed, accessible to more students than the ones I work with one-on-one. So I wrote *Surviving the College Application Process: Case Studies to Help You Find Your Unique Angle for Success.* There are many preexisting resources that tell students *what* to do in a step-by-step guide. However, almost none of them show students the *why* and the *how* of the application process. The purpose of this book is to take the guesswork out of identifying what is important and why it is important. I have done this by providing eleven real-life case studies of students who faced a similar task as you: not only trying to find the college that fit them the best, but also figuring out how best to communicate that compatibility to the college.

A NOTE TO STUDENTS:
HOW THIS BOOK WILL HELP YOU GET INTO COLLEGE

- You will learn how to approach the process at every stage, from the start of high school through your senior year, when you are actually applying to college.
- You will have a clear roadmap for the college application process by seeing real examples of how other students did it.
- You will understand how to match your strengths with a list of colleges that will value your strengths.
- You will walk away knowing how to think strategically about your application, which will help you develop a stronger application for each college.
- You will understand *how* and *why* to focus on specific areas of your profile, based on what makes you stand out.

- You will be able to see aspects of yourself in the student case studies, and apply what you learn from them to your own application or college plan.
- You will be able to understand how all the pieces of your application come together—the personal statement, the brag sheet, the supplemental essays, arts supplement, and so forth—to create a strong story about you for college admissions boards.

Ultimately, you will have the tools to not only survive but thrive throughout the entire college application process.

My hope is that in reading these case studies, you will be able to relate to one or more of the students profiled. I have also provided questions to ask yourself at the end of each case study to help you identify what is important for you. These are the types of questions that my associates and I have asked the hundreds of clients whom we have helped through the process. We have numerous resources available on our website, collegeboundmentor.com, along with our *On the Road with College Bound Mentor* blog that profiles colleges we visit to help make the right match for our clients. You can read through these college visit profiles and identify if a school seems like a good fit for you at collegeboundmentor.com/blog.

PART 1

WHAT'S AN ANGULAR STUDENT AND WHY SHOULD YOU WANT TO BE ONE?

CHAPTER 1

THE ANGULAR STUDENT

An angular student is a student who possesses a well-demonstrated depth or degree of excellence in one or two areas—leadership, intellectual curiosity, athletics, or community service—or who has a special talent or exhibits unusual personal character. Parents might recognize this focus on the angle a student brings to the application process as something new when compared with the relevant emphasis that was touted when they applied to college. And they would be right.

In the early eighties, when I myself applied, the buzzword for college acceptance was "well-rounded," which referred to a student who participated in many different activities. That is no longer what colleges are looking for from applicants. Now they want to build a well-rounded class made up of students who will each fill one or two slices of their total round pie: in other words, students who are unique, focused, and angular (or express excellence or uniqueness) in their interests. In fact, according to a recent *New York Times* article, "Such students are known in college admissions circles as 'pointy'—being well-rounded doesn't cut it anymore. You need to have a spike in your achievement chart."

To respond to what colleges are looking for now, I developed what I call the College Application Wheel. It acts as a framework and a tool that helps students feel in control of this sometimes confusing process. It will not only assist you in identifying your strengths and "gaps"—areas that you may need to fill in such as community service or higher standardized test scores—it will also help you identify where your energy may best be spent in making yourself shine or stand out from the crowd. It will help you understand what makes you unique, how to find a college that values you for who you are, and help you see where there is a match between you and a specific college.

The College Application Wheel

The key components of the College Application Wheel are:

- Academics/test scores
- Extracurricular activities
- Leadership
- Intellectual curiosity
- Athletics
- Special talents
- Financial
- Other

Colleges don't expect you to excel in all eight of these categories, but they do look at these areas to determine if you will be a good academic, cultural, emotional, financial, and character-based "fit" with their institution.

Let's look a little more specifically at what colleges want to see from their applicants. While academics and test scores get you into the game, they are no longer enough to ensure that you will be a successful player. However, as you'll soon learn, the wheel, and the traits within it, can tip the scales in your favor. Colleges want to create a community of learners and assemble a group of students who will collectively make up a well-rounded class. Knowing what pieces of the college's wheel you fill out and what your angle is will help you find the right fit between them and you.

Okay, so how do you decide which pieces apply to you? Each of the eight parts or spokes of the wheel deserves your attention, because, taken together, they will help you understand where to focus your energy. For instance, if you are not athletic, that segment of the wheel will not apply to you, and that is okay. However, the wheel has two parts. The first part is to understand which segments are your strengths, and the second part is to know how to link these assets to the needs of the college. In other words, you want to help the college you choose see how you will positively contribute to its campus life given your strengths according to the wheel. Taking this one step further, it is only through a thorough examination of your alignment with the wheel and the college's alignment with the wheel that you will be able to select the right college for you.

This book will walk you through the process of developing a strategic plan for high school and, later on, for applying to college. It will also provide case studies of real students who used this approach to develop their own plans and successfully apply to colleges that valued their strengths.

You will meet the following angular students in the case studies included in part 2:

- Noah, a gifted actor from suburban New Jersey with strong intellectual curiosity, used the summer between junior and senior year to explore his interest in politics and Judaism; this experience helped him stand out. He also used his special talent in theater as a complementary angle. He had above-average grades, curriculum, and SAT scores. Noah was accepted early decision to the College of William and Mary.

- Feydi, a highly competitive first-generation Nigerian American student from a large suburban high school, used her multicultural background, hard work, athletics, and interest in science to secure a scholarship at multiple schools. She had solid SAT scores and needed financial assistance so she would have enough money for medical school. She was accepted to multiple schools, including an Ivy League school, with need-based and merit-based financial aid.

- Kyle, an athlete turned actor, lacked confidence to accept a position on the varsity soccer team during his sophomore year, so he remained on the junior varsity team. That year, the varsity soccer team won the state tournament. He used his regret to fuel his newly developed special talent for acting. Whereas he let his fears control him in soccer, in acting, he was determined to push through his fears and take risks. He also realized that he needed to push himself further academically and personally to achieve his goals. He had above-average grades, but needed a more rigorous curriculum. His SAT scores did not match his grades. He needed financial assistance, which we factored into his overall strategy. Kyle was accepted to multiple schools with merit aid.

- Hayley found her angle by tying her committee work in Model UN on the environment to her interest in math and science. Hayley had above-average grades with a challenging curriculum and excellent SATs. Hayley was unsure of what she wanted to study in college, vacillating between business, pre-med, and possibly engineering. She attended a six-week pre-college summer program designed to prepare students for majors in engineering, pre-med, or technology called PAVE at Vanderbilt University to explore all three areas. After the summer, she was leaning toward business because she did not really see an area of engineering that interested her. However, after researching programs at her schools of interest, she hit on environmental engineering, something to which she could relate based on her experience with Model UN. She used this combination of interests to create her angle and gain admission into several select universities.

- Dan, a devoted jazz musician, top student, and leader, found his angle through his special talent and leadership within music and the Junior Statesmen of America club. He had high grades and test scores, but he also wanted to major in music, so he needed to impress the music professors as well. He applied early action to the University of North Carolina at Chapel Hill and the University of Virginia, but got deferred to both and then waitlisted. He used his connections with a music professor to secure a spot off of the waitlist.

- Kaden, a transgender social activist filmmaker with a few academic bumps and average test scores, found his angle through switching focus from politics to film and narrating his own transformation on YouTube. He also started a series of student run meet-ups for other LBGTQ students in the area. His angles were leadership, special talent, and other. He started at community college and then transferred to film school at SUNY Purchase after the first year.

- Jenny, a talented, multisport athlete who overcame some personal adversity, used her athletic talent to get recruited at a small liberal arts college. She had above-average grades, curriculum, and test scores, but needed financial assistance to attend college. She was accepted early decision to Ursinus College with merit aid.

- Adam, a super science nerd who was super strong in math and science but weak in language, stood out by finding his place within the scientific community in a lab in Greece. He highlighted his intellectual curiosity by describing how he finally fit in. He also overcame an illness and learning difference, which he highlighted in his additional information. He was accepted to multiple schools.

- Francesca, a closet computer science nerd and popular athlete, used her intellectual curiosity in a typically male-dominated field to find her angle. She had outstanding grades and test scores in a highly competitive curriculum. She initially feared that her friends would make fun of her for enjoying computer science, but ultimately she found a way to show them how cool computer science and coding can be. She was accepted early decision to an Ivy League college.

- Hugh, a scientist by day and theater aficionado by night from a stereotypical Asian family, used his dual interests to separate himself from the pack and convince his parents that there were multiple roads to success. He applied to accelerated medical (BAMD) programs as well as numerous colleges with liberal arts curriculums. He had a highly rigorous schedule with good grades and strong test scores, but they were not strong enough for the BAMD programs. Although he got an interview for an accelerated program, his heart was elsewhere. He was accepted to numerous colleges, including a highly selective top-ten liberal arts college.

- Veema, a sensitive multicultural writer and social activist, found her angle by using her special talent in writing as a vehicle to overcome adversity. She had below-average grades with an above-average curriculum and test scores. She had a learning difference and needed financial assistance. She used her special talent, leadership, and "other" category on the College Application Wheel by documenting the many changes in her life during the early part of high school to show how she had grown personally and academically. She was accepted to multiple schools with merit aid.

2

POWERING UP YOUR COLLEGE APPLICATION WHEEL

Here is how you can use the College Application Wheel at every stage of your application process.

As a freshman or sophomore in high school, you can use the wheel to develop your own strategic plan based on your strengths. You can read through what other students have done and get some ideas for designing your own path. (Parents, you can use this tool to help your student think through a strategic plan for high school.)

As a junior, you can begin to identify some schools that are a good fit for you academically, socially, and emotionally. You can see how and why other students created their college lists based on their wheel, and these can provide a roadmap for your own journey. (Parents, you can help your student think through his needs and find a college that is a great fit.)

As a senior, you can figure out how best to present yourself to colleges and communicate the match between you and each school. You can find similarities between you and the case study students to see how best to communicate your unique strengths to your chosen colleges. (Parents, you can look objectively at your student's talents and help her present her unique strengths.)

The case studies in this book describe students with varied backgrounds, interests, and aspirations. You will most likely find aspects of yourself in one or more of these case studies, and you can use those similarities to help you plan your own application strategy.

Now, let's look more closely at the eight segments of the College Application Wheel.

Academics/Test Scores

Your grades, the degree of challenge present in your high school curriculum (known as "rigor"), and your SAT/ACT scores form the most important section of the College Application Wheel. The reason is simple: These numbers are the best way to reveal your capability and progress. Ultimately, academic rigor and achievement, test scores, and grades provide you with the best chance for gaining access to the colleges of your choice.

However, numbers aren't everything for applying to college. Remember that aside from grades and test scores, choosing the right college is all about finding the place where you feel like you belong. National college rankings, your grades and test scores, student populations, and other numbers tell you little about the best college match for your personality, pursuits, and career goals. At the end of the day, you should ask yourself a single question about choosing a college: Are my skills, passions, and experiences in alignment with the colleges that I'm interested in attending?

Most important, you should be challenging yourself appropriately, improving your grades and test scores, and learning about your abilities and capabilities. Along those lines, here are some questions:

- How can I improve my grades in my weakest subjects?
- Have I gone in for extra help from my teachers?
- Am I challenging myself appropriately? Do I have enough honors, Advanced Placement, or International Baccalaureate classes? Do I have too many?

- Should I find a study partner at school?
- Should I get a tutor to help me with weaker subjects?
- Should I take SAT and ACT training sessions?
- Am I working to my full capacity, or can I work harder?

Other important questions might include:

- At which college can I develop the skills I need to pursue my passion?
- Will a given school prepare me for acceptance into a graduate school or to get a job?
- At which school would I best fit—and be happiest?
- Will the colleges I'm considering challenge my intellectual curiosity?
- Considering my grades, am I being realistic about the schools to which I'm applying?
- What are the freshmen retention rates (the percentage of freshmen who return for their sophomore year) at the schools to which I'm applying? A high retention rate can reveal overall student satisfaction.
- Can I improve my test scores to gain admission to my dream school? If so, how can I do that?

Extracurricular Activities

Extracurricular activities are another important segment that can set you apart and help you become an angular student. In addition to stellar grades and exemplary SAT and ACT scores, colleges seek students who have demonstrated leadership and social skills through extracurricular activities, such as school clubs and groups. But they prefer to see depth in one or two areas. This means that you don't need to join a million clubs simply to bulk up your activities.

That said, extracurricular activities are, by definition, anything you do outside of high school courses. Extracurricular activities include temple/

church groups, local theater troupes, work, musical groups, or being an arts scene aficionado. Broaden your definition of extracurricular activities—beyond school-sponsored groups such as yearbook, band, or football—to include community and family activities. Taking part in extracurricular activities tells college admissions officers that a student not only has the academic skills to succeed, but also has the community spirit that colleges want.

To find out if you have the right stuff, ask yourself these questions:

- Have I joined any community or temple/church groups?
- Am I involved in the arts—such as theater, music, dance, painting, photography, creative writing, or other creative endeavors?
- Do I belong to any school clubs—such as math, bowling, chess, or Spanish club?
- Have I become involved in any community activities, including fundraising, event organizing, or even manning a booth at a temple/church fair?
- Do I play on a sports team?
- Do I perform any volunteer work?

Involvement in extracurricular activities can also allow the prospective college student to do some soul-searching about how devoted he is to certain pursuits. Colleges always like to see grit and passion in any endeavor. With that in mind, ask yourself these questions:

- Have I pushed myself to take advantage of opportunities that come my way?
- Have I joined a club that involves some public speaking—e ven though, like the majority of people, I'm terrified of public speaking?
- Have I joined activities that have brought me deeper into my passions?

- Have I pushed myself beyond my comfort zone? For example, have I joined activities that have forced me into socializing with other students?

Leadership

Students often possess leadership qualities of which they're not even aware, perhaps stemming from experiences they may discount because they do not realize that leaders emerge to fill many roles. Obvious leadership roles include being captain of a sports team or being an elected class officer. Other leadership traits and experiences can include being a manager at a part-time job, spearheading a fundraising effort, organizing a school club, belonging to a school committee, organizing a school trip, or starting an intramural sports team. Leadership can also take the form of standing up for something in which you believe, writing a blog, or mentoring others.

The following questions might help you discover your leadership abilities:

- Are you the captain of a sports team? Can you become one? What will it take?
- Are you the president or head of a club or organization? Can you become one? What will you need to do?
- Did you found a club or organize any student activity?
- Did you become a manager in a part-time or a summer job?
- Did you get a part in a school play?
- Did you head up a crew for a school play—lighting, makeup, costumes, set design?
- Are you section leader in the school band?
- Did you organize an event at your school?
- Have you taken a leadership role in your own family? Family leadership can include helping out with a sick sibling or other family member. Perhaps you helped your parents care for younger siblings?
- Have you tutored peers or younger kids in a particular area?

- Do you have your own lawn mowing, gardening, or snowplowing business? If so, did you invest your own money in your business?
- Do you have a hobby—for example, coin, stamp, or antique collecting—that involves buying and selling and/or belonging to an organization?

Intellectual Curiosity

Sometimes it's hard to quantify a student's intellectual curiosity—that is, until she joins a club or activity, or actually creates a project or product. Intellectual curiosity can be an important segment in the College Application Wheel, and many Ivy League and other highly selective colleges—such as Harvard University, Yale University, the University of Chicago, and Stanford University—expect students to possess an expansive intellectual curiosity supported by their general knowledge, books they've read, and research they've undertaken. An intellectually curious student might possess the motivation to solve arcane engineering problems, to write a story or an article, to write a research paper analyzing social trends, to create a sculpture, or perhaps even to write computer code. A college essay can be the best place to document the products of your intellectual curiosity by showing how you think and why something interests you.

Here are some questions that might help you discern your own intellectual curiosity:

- Do you read at least one newspaper or news website each day?
- Do you subscribe to any trade magazines or to any science or engineering magazines?
- Have you created your own website? Your own blog?
- Are you involved in any of the arts—music, dance, painting, theater, writing, or so forth? How are you involved?
- Are you generally intellectually curious about life? That is, do you routinely search the Internet to learn about new technology, phenomena, people, places, or events?

- Do you download and listen to educational podcasts or iTunes University courses?
- Have you participated in any pre-college summer programs to go deeper in an area of interest such as engineering, visual or performing arts, creative writing, or politics?
- Are you a member of Model UN, Youth and Government, DECA, Science Olympiad, or other academic-related clubs?
- Have you traveled to other countries, either on your own or through exchange programs? What have you learned about other cultures and countries?
- Are you a big reader? Who are some of your favorite authors?
- Do you follow the stock market? Have you invested any of your own money?
- Are you part of a football or basketball fantasy league? Do you research players and analyze their statistics?

Athletics

Many students participate in sports, though few are talented enough to be recruited athletes. However, if you are talented enough, athletics will make up the largest piece of your wheel in terms of time and commitment. Team sports offer more than just a chance to excel athletically. Teammates learn to work together toward a goal—and also learn a lot about winning, losing, and how to play the game.

The following questions might help you measure your achievement in sports:

- Are you a star player on your high school team? Have you made it to an all-county or all-state team? Are you nationally ranked?
- Do you play varsity sports in high school?
- Do you play any sports in high school? Have you earned a letter or any other awards?
- Do you play on any intramural teams?

If you are an exceptional high school athlete, you will need to think about how much you want to pursue the sport in college. Do you want to play Division I or II sports, in which you are an athlete first, but you can get an athletic scholarship? Or would you prefer to be a student first and forego the athletic scholarship while playing Division III sports? Most schools also offer club and intramural sports. The same applies to playing in a school marching band or being a cheerleader—smaller schools allow students to be a big fish in a smaller pond.

With this in mind, you might consider the following questions:

- Have you employed your athletic abilities to their fullest extent?
- Will you have the time, passion, commitment, and ability to play on a team in college?
- Have you made contact with the appropriate coaches at the appropriate time?
- Are you attending athletic showcases or summer sports camps for your sport that will expose you to college coaches at the schools that interest you?
- Do you have an athletic resume?
- Have you registered for the NCAA Eligibility Center or on individual college athletics websites?
- Do you want to play Division I, II, or III athletics? How much will sports play into your decision?
- Will you be satisfied playing club or intramural sports?
- What happens if you get injured? Will you still like the college if you can't play the sport?
- What coaches are interested in you? Do these schools align with your other interests?
- How can you get more coaches to know about you?

Special Talents

Students with special talents in the visual or performing arts can use this angle in a number of ways. For a student who wants to pursue a bachelor of fine arts or a bachelor of music degree, there is typically an audition component that counts for as much as 50 percent of the decision. For students who do not want to major in their special talent, colleges still value these talents tremendously because most colleges need students to join their musical groups, plays, dance troupes, and arts organizations. A special talent can add an extra arrow to an applicant's quiver. For example, an engineering student applying to MIT might impress an admissions board if he plays fiddle in an old-time band or won an essay contest.

It may also be important to remember that special talents can include a wide spectrum of abilities—from singing, to debating ability, to mathematical ability, to a facility with foreign languages, to playing a musical instrument, to acting, to mechanical construction, to computer programming, to student politics, even to a desire to help others.

Describing a quirky talent on a college application is a fine idea—particularly if you can share the creativity behind your special talent and show how it has helped define you. One student, for instance, wrote his essay about riding a unicycle on the boardwalk and how it helped him overcome his shyness by becoming an entertainer. Colleges are most interested in seeing if you've actually developed and employed your special talents.

To discover whether you've done that, ask yourself these questions:

- Do I play a musical instrument?
- Can I sing well?
- Do I write better than the average student?
- Has my writing been published? Do I write a blog? Have I written skits for talent shows?
- Have I gone deep into any of my passions?
- Have I joined activities that have fostered my talent?
- Have I displayed my special talents to others?
- Have my talents actually produced a tangible product or process?
- How would I best employ my talent in college?
- Do I speak a foreign language?

- How will I contribute these talents to a college community?
- Am I a whiz at Photoshop, Blender, Illustrator, or other design software programs?
- Do I play guitar or sing with a rock band?
- Can I juggle?
- Can I ride a unicycle or a horse?

Financial

The investment parents and students make in education is astronomical. In fact, only the family home is a bigger financial investment. But in terms of its return on investment, education is truly the most important investment of your life.

However, there's another related point that is important to remember. While it is true that college costs a lot of money, don't scratch a school off your list because of sticker shock. Many expensive schools offer excellent financial aid packages to attract students from different income levels.

To make use of financial aid, parents need to have a frank talk with their teenagers about what their family is able to pay and the amount the student is expected to contribute. Then figure out how much financial aid you need for every school you are considering, being sure to factor in books, housing, transportation, meals, and other incidentals when you estimate the total cost.

If you and your family feel blindsided by the increasingly high cost of college, remember that many scholarships exist for those who need financial aid.

Colleges generally take one of the following three approaches with regard to admissions and financial aid:

- **Need-blind:** They do not consider an applicant's ability to pay when making a decision.
- **Accept/deny:** They accept students; however, they do not offer much (or any) need-based aid, which could make it impossible for some students to attend.

- **Need-sensitive:** They factor the student's ability to pay when making admissions decisions. They can determine this through zip codes and parents' professions, even if a student does not submit an application for financial aid.

These three approaches aside, it has become increasingly difficult for schools to remain need-blind, given the prolonged economic downturn. So if you need financial aid to attend college, it is important to have a clear strategy when developing your list of schools. Families should understand their expected family contribution (EFC) based on the FAFSA (federal forms) and CSS Profile (institutional method). The EFC is the amount of money a given college calculates that your family can contribute toward your education. You should research which schools will meet a student's full demonstrated need. Schools that meet full demonstrated need will provide need-based financial aid for the difference between the total cost of attendance minus the EFC. Schools that do not meet full demonstrated need often "gap" financial aid, meaning that they do not provide the full difference between total cost of attendance and the family's EFC. Each school now provides a net price calculator on its financial aid website to help families determine their EFC and how much financial aid they may receive. Our website, collegeboundmentor.com, provides links to a net price calculator under Resources. However, this is only an estimate. Each school will determine your need a bit differently.

When providing assistance, most schools provide a blended award to families composed of the following:

- Gifts (institutional, federal, and merit grants that do not have to be paid back)
- Work-study program assistance
- Loans (only subsidized loans are considered aid because interest does not start accruing until the student graduates)

If you do not need financial aid to attend college, you may have a distinct advantage in the third category of schools, those that are need-sensitive. This is an opportunity for you as a full-pay student to apply to a school and have an increased likelihood of acceptance, provided it is a good fit. For these lucky students, the ability to pay may become part of their angle.

If you do not qualify for need-based financial aid, do not despair, because many colleges also offer merit-based aid. Merit-based aid is awarded solely on a student's merit and does not take financial need into account. A good resource for finding schools that offer merit aid is meritaid.com. There are also a number of schools that offer scholarships for special talents in many different areas. Scholarships exist for musical performance, leadership skills, community service, and many other areas. That special talent of yours may actually help you pay for school. Some schools offer significant merit scholarships for talents like music, creative abilities, or entrepreneurship, as well as stellar grades and test scores. Many talent-based scholarships can provide up to $10,000 toward a college education—so it's really worth the time involved in researching these scholarships to see if you might qualify.

However, if, like most students, you don't get a scholarship to a school, you have to answer certain financial questions:

- Can your family afford a private, away-from-home school? If you are a full-pay student, at which schools will that help you to get accepted?
- Do you qualify for any merit scholarships? Spend time researching scholarship opportunities and identify at least seven to pursue.
- Can you afford the debt of student loans? Factor the entire debt compared to your income opportunity once you've graduated. Be aware that your goals may change over four years. Are you willing to assume this debt? A good rule of thumb is to take on no more than two-thirds of your anticipated first-year salary. So if you anticipate making $45,000 your first year, then you should take on no more than $30,000 for the entire four years of college.
- Would you be willing to contribute to the cost of your education? List five ways that you could contribute.

- Are there work-study opportunities?
- Do you plan on going to graduate school? How will you pay for that?

Other

"Other" can mean almost anything that doesn't neatly fit into a student's life-experience box when applying to a college. These other skills, talents, and experiences can add weight to a college application and impress an admissions board. Admissions officers realize it's often difficult to quantify a student's full capacity based on grades, test scores, and extracurricular activities alone, so other achievements can add yet another point of differentiation.

"Other" can include things like being a member of an underrepresented minority, representing geographic diversity, being a first-generation college student, being a legacy student (going to the same school from which one of your parents graduated), being a student who overcame adversity, being a student who has demonstrated strength of character, coming from a multicultural background, having an international background, or choosing to study a subject in which your gender or ethnicity is underrepresented.

Questions about the "other" category that students should answer include:

- Are you a legacy at any universities—that is, did your parents and/or grandparents attend that school?
- Are you interested in a field that is typically more weighted by the opposite gender—such as a male interested in nursing, or a female interested in engineering?
- Are you the first person in your family to attend college?
- Are you willing to travel to an area in the country that is not well represented by your state?
- Have you overcome adversity? How did you respond? Can you show strength of character?

- Are you an underrepresented minority—for example, African American, Native American, Hispanic?

In the end, to say that the decision about which college to attend will shape your destiny might be a bit melodramatic. However, it is still irrefutable that where you spend these formative years will shape the direction of your life and the connections you make, and become the foundation for your career.

How can you apply this information to your own applications? The student case studies that follow will give you clear examples of how you can apply the College Application Wheel to yourself and your own life.

Use these as examples in making your own decisions, but do not use them as a blueprint. You, like every student, have unique talents, abilities, and desires that are unlike anyone else's. Just as no two colleges are alike, the same is true for the students who attend them, so be sure to create your own unique college application plan.

These real-life case studies were drawn from my independent college consulting practice, and each case profiles a student who found his or her angle, despite very different academic and personal goals. Finding someone to whom you can relate will help you create a path that is both realistic and achievable.

CHAPTER 3

ADDING SOME APPS TO YOUR COLLEGE APPLICATION

Getting In: What's Marketing Got to Do with It?

Before I founded College Bound Mentor and began to live and breathe the world of college, I spent more than fifteen years in marketing. I started off as a product manager for a medical device firm, worked as a consultant to numerous companies such as Coach and AutoTrader. com, served as director of recruiting for Ticketmaster Online/City Search, and taught marketing full time at Whittier College. I realized that just as a product or service can be differentiated from other products or services with its unique selling proposition (USP), students have a unique selling proposition, too—one that will make them attractive to the right school. Now that you have gone through the College Application Wheel, hopefully you have a better idea of what your USP or your angle is. The college application is your place to market yourself and communicate your USP or angle to prospective colleges. Each piece of the application tells admissions a different part of your story, so the key is to make every part of your application shine. It all starts with your personal statement.

The Personal Statement: Finding Your Voice

The personal statement is another name for your main essay. Meeting with my clients to brainstorm for their personal statements is among my favorite parts of the process. I get to delve into the depths of my clients' lives and help them think about how best to tell their stories. I am always amazed by their varied experiences and how they approach life differently depending on their interests and background.

However, the personal statement is also the most challenging part of the application process for most students. Up until now, the bulk of your writing has been in the form of analytical nonfiction essays about books you read or perhaps answering document-based questions for history class. Many of my students struggle with what they should write about because they don't know exactly what they want to communicate. And of those seventeen-year-olds who know what they want to say about themselves, very few know how to tell it in a compelling, interesting way. The personal statement not only must be compelling and interesting, but it should also convey your voice and personality in 250–650 words.

No wonder it's so hard! But it doesn't have to be if you ask yourself the right questions.

So, what are some keys questions to ask yourself before you sit down to write your unique story?

- **What are your strengths and weaknesses?** Most people have something to overcome, something that makes them different from their peers. How did you grapple with a weakness or accommodate for a weakness with your strengths? The specifics of a story are what make for an interesting essay. You will read about Kaden (case study 6), a transgender teen who wanted to make a difference in the world. Before Kaden physically transitioned to being male, he thought politics was where he could make a difference, but he realized that politics was all about appearances.

Instead, he turned to film and used his creativity and activist voice toward a medium better suited for his strengths.

- **What are your key themes?** Everyone has certain themes that run through his or her life. It could be that you enjoy working with kids, that you never quite fit in with your peers, or that you seek and enjoy challenges in academics and athletics. Think about themes that cross over into various parts of your life and find a way to illustrate that theme through a particular story or series of events. In Dan's instance (case study 5), music and leadership were themes that ran through his life. He integrated the two in everything that he did.

- **What is your inciting incident?** In the literary world, every story has an inciting incident. This is the incident that sets the story in motion. So think about your own life and identify if there is one event that caused you to think about yourself or the world differently. It could be suffering an injury that prevented you from playing sports, almost losing your first job because you forgot to tell your boss you wouldn't be in, or something as seemingly mundane as watching a program on television that sparked your interest. The key is to show the reader how and why this event impacted you. For Adam (case study 8), getting sick and not being able to take his ADHD medication became the inciting incident that pushed him forward and made him reach his full potential in school.

- **What do you want to communicate?** Once you determine your topic, think about what you want the admissions officer to think about you after he has read your application. It should tie back to your strengths and weaknesses. The personal statement is the opportunity to go beyond what is listed in your application and learn more about what drives you. What makes you tick? Why do you think the way you do? What anecdote will best communicate how you approach the world? Francesca (case study 9) wanted to communicate how she thinks in code, even though at first she didn't think it made her appear cool. Her case study showed us how she not only overcame her initial embarrassment but also changed the way she viewed her own education and place among her peers.

The Common Application (commonapp.org), a centralized application that can be submitted to multiple schools, requires students to submit one personal statement with a minimum of 250 words and a maximum of 650 words. The essay prompts are:

- Some students have a background or story that is so central to their identity that they believe their application would be incomplete without it. If this sounds like you, then please share your story.
- Recount an incident or time when you experienced failure. How did it affect you, and what lessons did you learn?
- Reflect on a time when you challenged a belief or idea. What prompted you to act? Would you make the same decision again?
- Describe a place or environment where you are perfectly content. What do you do or experience there, and why is it meaningful to you?
- Discuss an accomplishment or event, formal or informal, that marked your transition from childhood to adulthood within your culture, community, or family.

You can find the prompts for colleges not on the Common Application on their websites. But I would worry less about the prompts and more about your story and how to connect to the reader in a personal way.

The Detailed Activity Listing: How Do You Spend Your Time?

The Common Application provides an area to outline your activities. (Most non–Common Application schools do as well.) This is your opportunity to describe in a very specific way how you spend your time. You will have several drop-down menus to indicate the type of activity—athletic, student government, community service, and so on.

Many students identify the activity but do not explain their involvement in any detail. This is a mistake. Just as you want your personal statement to connect with the reader on the how and why, the detailed activity listing is your opportunity to show prospective colleges what you have done and the depth of your involvement. So, just as you should brainstorm before you sit down to write your personal statement, you should also write down all your activities and summarize the specifics of your involvement. For example, if you are captain of a sports team, what did you do in that role? If you organized a fundraiser, what was it for and how much did you raise? If you founded an organization that you call SMAC, what does SMAC stand for? You can be certain that an admissions counselor will not know that SMAC stands for Students' Movement Against Cancer.

You may have the opportunity to provide a more detailed brag sheet in the school- specific supplement for schools on the Common Application. This is an opportunity to showcase your involvement in more detail and carve out your angle by how you group your activities. For example, Noah (case study 1) organized his activities by performing arts (special talent) and community service. In the performing arts section he included his role in all the shows that he performed in through school and summer camp as well as his involvement in chorus. In the community service section he went into detail on his leadership roles in the Jewish community.

Letters of Recommendation: Your Backup Voice

The Common Application requires academic letters of recommendation and also allows for supplemental letters from coaches, bosses, clergy, arts teachers, and so on. For the academic letters, you should choose teachers from your academic subjects (math, science, foreign language, English, social studies, theology), ideally ones who taught you during your sophomore or junior year. The teachers who write your academic letters of recommendation should be able to describe your contributions to the classroom. As an added bonus, teachers who have personally observed you outside of the classroom as a coach or club advisor can speak to your contribution to the larger school community.

If you have a special talent, are interested in majoring in a visual or performing art, or are interested in attending an art school or conservatory, you should also ask a teacher from that discipline who has worked closely with you or has had the opportunity to observe your talent. This can be included in the supplemental letters section on the Common Application or sent directly to the college for other applications.

I heard David Weisbord, the associate director of admissions at Columbia University, speak to a group of guidance counselors on the importance of their letters of recommendation in helping a student stand out. He put together a top-ten list of areas he likes to see addressed in letters of recommendation. He stressed that he did not expect that every letter include all ten areas, but, just as with the College Application Wheel, finding the key areas that define the student makes a difference. His top ten areas are as follows:

10) Academic and non-academic strengths
   - In which subjects does the student stand out?
   - Does the student have a special talent?
9) Role models
   - Who are the student's role models—teachers, politicians, artists, family members, athletes?
8) Demonstration of strong character and maturity
   - Has the student overcome life adversity?
   - Is the student an effective handler of stress and time?
   - What family obligations does the student have?
7) Assertive or laid-back
   - How likely is the student to thrive in a certain environment?
   - Is the student a change agent?
6) Student's best work in the classroom
   - Was there a defining paper, research project, science lab work, or art work?
5) Intellectual curiosity
   - Is the student a voracious reader?
   - Does he take any independent study classes?

- Is she a learner of foreign languages?
- Does the student enroll in college courses for personal enrichment and not for college?

4) Embrace diversity on college campus environment
   - Does the student have an active voice for diversity?
   - Does he interact with different people?
   - Is she open-minded?

3) High school and community service
   - Does the student do it for personal reasons or just to get into college?
   - Did the student found a club?
   - Was there a four-year commitment?
   - Was there a summer commitment too?

2) Leadership without a title
   - Did the student lose an election but stay active in the club?
   - Did she organize a food or clothing drive?
   - Did he do clerical work?
   - Did the student promote school spirit?

1) Left their mark
   - Will you remember this student a few years after graduation?
   - Was he a role model to freshmen and sophomores?
   - Can we expect the same commitment on the collegiate level?

As you can see, these areas closely mirror the College Application Wheel, so the better you can do at providing your teachers and guidance counselors with specific material to highlight what makes you unique, the better they can corroborate your strengths. That is how your letters of recommendation can serve as important complementary angles to your application.

Supplemental Essays

Each school that participates in the Common Application has the ability to request supplemental essays ranging from a short answer (150 words) to a longer essay (500 words, or in some cases no limit). The most common supplemental essay questions are "Why this school?" and "Why this academic interest?" Many admissions professionals say that they read the "Why this school?" essay first. They want to see if you as an applicant truly know why you want to attend the school other than its excellent reputation, outstanding location, or world-renowned faculty. I often ask students to do the brochure test. If it looks like what you wrote came straight out of the college's brochure or website, then go back to the drawing board.

This essay is a chance for you to make the match between your interests and talents and the school's offerings. Veema (case study 11) chose only small liberal arts colleges that emphasized creativity and strong interaction between students and faculty. When she wrote her "Why this school?" essay for Allegheny College, she identified specific classes (Medieval and Renaissance studies) and clubs (political and LBGTQ) that interested her. She also wove in anecdotes from her visit to show how comfortable she felt with the professors and students. She made it easy for an admissions committee to see her thriving and contributing to the school community.

The "Why this academic interest?" essay provides you an opportunity to show your intellectual curiosity. Even if you do not know what you want to major in, you can identify some areas of interest and why. Hayley (case study 4) described how she became interested in environmental engineering through her involvement with the energy committee at Model UN. She combined her strength in math and science with her interest in creating sustainable energy solutions. She then identified specific courses and programs at each school that would help her achieve her goal. She was even able to adapt this academic interest essay for Lehigh University's prompt "If you could create your own university, what would it focus on?" She talked about her interest in sustainable energy and how she would design an interdisciplinary curriculum around solving this problem.

Other supplemental essay questions can run the gamut and often reflect the values of the school. However, even though essay prompts may seem totally unrelated, if you think about what you want to communicate, you can often find a way to adapt an essay to fit multiple prompts. Hugh (case study 10) was able to tweak his essay on breaking away from the Asian stereotype and pressure imposed by his parents for seven seemingly disparate essay prompts, from Amherst College's prompt ("Stereotyped beliefs have the power to become self-fulfilling prophesies for behavior"), to Boston College's prompt ("Tell us about a time you had all of the facts but missed the meaning"), to the University of Michigan's prompt ("Choose one of the communities to which you belong, and describe your place within it").

For Amherst's prompt, Hugh emphasized how he broke away from the stereotyped beliefs of his parents that all Asians should focus only on work and not on outside interests. He rejected this notion and realized that there is much more to life than work, and he described how he found joy in New York City. For Boston College, he adapted this to talk about how he had been focusing only on the facts his parents told him about success, but in doing so, he missed the meaning of life, which is to find passion in the arts, sports, and other areas. Finally, for the University of Michigan, he described his Asian community and showed how his role was to lead his parents to a larger view of the world. In each instance, Hugh showed his leadership and his intellectual curiosity. He served as a change agent in his community and would continue to do so while in college.

So, before you write each of your supplemental essays separately, see if there is a common theme that draws them together. Then think about what you want to communicate and how you can adapt one or two essays to fit the prompts, rather than writing a separate essay for each supplement.

Athletic Resume

An athletic resume is often sent to coaches before your application if you are a recruited athlete. In this resume you want to include the key metrics for your sport—for example, height and weight for basketball and volleyball, times for swimming and track, USTA ranking for tennis, and so on. If you have not already been recruited, some Division III schools may still have openings in their roster.

Jenny (case study 7), a recruited athlete for basketball and possibly volleyball, sent an athletic resume including her height and weight, her upcoming tournaments, high school and club team information, and various awards she received. This allowed the coach from Ursinus to identify her as a potential recruit before she even applied.

While Kyle (case study 3) did not intend to play soccer in college, he grouped his activities on his brag sheet under performing arts, where he showcased his acting credits; athletics, where he highlighted his soccer accolades; and community service, where he detailed his volunteer work. This allowed admissions committees to ascertain very quickly where he would make his mark on campus.

Audition/Performing Arts DVD, CD, or Web Link

If your special talent plays heavily into your wheel, then you will likely have an audition or submit a sample of your work as part of the admission process. Noah (case study 1) did not intend to pursue performing arts as a major; however, he did want to showcase his work to admissions, so he included a five-minute DVD of his performances in the Arts Supplement of the Common Application. Kyle (case study 3) auditioned at Muhlenberg College so he could be eligible for a special talent scholarship.

Dan's (case study 5) music audition factored heavily into his admissions for the music schools. He set up auditions for all the schools and in some cases met with the instructors during his initial search and played for them informally. This allowed for the music professors to see his growth from junior to senior year. He also prepared an audio CD to submit to schools that required a CD instead of an audition.

When preparing for either an audition or a CD, make sure you know the specific requirements for each school. Those should be listed on their website under audition requirements. For example, do not prepare two jazz pieces when the requirements specify one jazz piece and one classical piece.

Each piece of your application tells your story, and your audition performance provides you an opportunity to showcase your special talent.

Art Portfolio

For artists, the art portfolio can count for 50 percent or more of your admissions score. Each school outlines on its website what is required for its portfolio. Many art schools also attend a National Portfolio Day event. If art is truly your passion and you are counting on your special talent to open the door to admissions, go to a National Portfolio Day event early on in your high school career. It will expose you to what other artists are doing and also put you in contact with admissions professionals from art schools, who can give you feedback on your work.

As you prepare your portfolio, make sure you have pieces that represent your true self and be ready to discuss what motivated you to create each piece. Just like in the personal statement, where the admissions committee wants to understand what drives you, in art, they want to get into your creative mindset and learn about your inspiration.

If you are talented artistically and plan on applying to an art school that requires a portfolio, you can still submit an art portfolio through the Arts Supplement on the Common Application using SlideRoom. If your art is in the form of creative writing, the arts supplement also provides an opportunity to submit samples of your writing.

Additional Information

This is the catch-all for anything else that you would like to submit. On the Common Application you have 650 words to include any additional information to support your application. Students should use this section to include anything that may have disrupted their education or explain (not excuse) their grades. It can also be used to highlight additional advanced placement or SAT subject tests, describe some research or an activity in more detail, or explain why a student transferred schools.

Veema (case study 11) used this section to outline her family situation and describe how she has managed her ADHD. Adam (case study 8) used this to describe why his grades dropped during sophomore year due to an illness and how he rebounded and had a different outlook on learning when he recovered. Jenny (case study 7) used this to describe why she transferred schools. In each case the students explained blips in their records, but did not make excuses.

PART 2

CASE STUDIES: STUDENT SUCCESS STORIES YOU CAN LEARN A LOT FROM

1

NOAH
THE INTELLECTUALLY CURIOUS ACTOR

Lessons Learned during the Application Process

In this case, you will learn how important it is to step outside your comfort zone and push yourself intellectually. Noah had spent six summers going to French Woods Festival, a theater arts camp, where he developed confidence and talent. However, he decided to take a different route for the summer between his junior and senior years to pursue one of his intellectual interests by attending a Jewish summer program that focused on politics and social action. This summer experience helped Noah grow intellectually and gave him insight on the type of academic environment that would interest him. It also gave him a context for showcasing his natural intellectual curiosity and ability to grow as a person.

Noah's Snapshot

- GPA: 3.86 (weighted, out of 4.3)
- Academic rigor: 10 honors/AP classes

- SAT: 1390/2050
- ACT: 30
- Class rank: top 25 percent

About Noah

- Main interests: history and theater
- Noah was intellectually curious.
- He wanted to be near a big city.
- He had an exceptional theater background.
- Selectivity and prestige of a school were important.

Personality Profile

Noah had two passions: history and theater. To him, they were interconnected in a way that might not be evident to a college admissions committee. His love of acting stemmed from his desire to understand and inhabit the minds of others, while his interest in history allowed him a context to imagine how he would act if he were in the shoes of a historical character. He approached the process of investing himself in a theatrical role similarly to an exercise in considering alternate perspectives.

He was a creative student with a sharp sense of humor. Noah acted boldly, spoke loudly, and was not afraid to make a fool of himself for effect or to prove a point. Even on the high school stage, Noah portrayed characters with a parallelism to his almost-larger-than-life personality and personal intensity—like Scrooge in *A Christmas Carol* and the Grinch in *Suessical the Musical.*

Creating Noah's College Application Wheel

I met Noah in February of his junior year. He was an accomplished high school actor and an above-average student with a rigorous schedule. It was easy to see his intellectual curiosity, involvement in his religious community, and natural talent in theater.

We identified a weakness in his community service. While Noah did volunteer sporadically, his heavy involvement in both the fall drama and the spring musical precluded volunteering in a significant way. In the back of my mind, I began thinking about how he could use the summer to make up for that missing piece in a way that linked to his natural interests.

I asked Noah how he usually spent his summers. Noah said that for the past six summers he had attended a performing arts camp in New York. It gave him a chance to excel at theatrical performance. He said summers at that camp greatly shaped his confidence through opportunities to meet like-minded friends. Of course, he planned on returning there for the entire summer before senior year.

I suggested that Noah use that summer to pursue his interest in politics and the Jewish community in greater depth in a way that would involve community service. I mentioned a particular program in Washington, DC, called Panim el Panim that could serve as a great option for meeting those goals.

His initial response was as expected: "What—you want me to give up going to camp, where I have spent the last six summers with all my friends and where I will be at the top of the food chain to spend four weeks in DC talking about politics and running a camp for underprivileged kids? Are you crazy?"

Okay, Noah did not say that, because he is too polite. Still, I imagine those thoughts ran through his head. In reality, Noah listened and promised to think about the idea. After several days and some parental encouragement, Noah opted for a more political and community service–oriented summer. He applied for the program and was accepted.

Noah's Strengths
- Natural intellectual curiosity
- Rigorous academic curriculum throughout high school
- Above-average test scores
- Some leadership experiences
- Legacy at the University of Pennsylvania and Brandeis University

Noah's Weaknesses

- Limited community service
- Few opportunities to explore his intellectual curiosity outside of school

Noah's Checklist

Noah had a strong academic record. His goal was to continue pushing himself academically and show a strong finish to his junior year and his first semester of senior year. Noah could take advantage of the summer to find opportunities for community service and enrich his intellectual curiosity. To stay true to his interests, I suggested that Noah should seriously consider a summer opportunity that could meld community service with interest in politics.

The Washington, DC, political program Panim el Panim was life-changing for Noah. He got to explore his interest in politics and gained experience with community service connected to his passions. And more important, the program and the people positively called into question his personal beliefs and political viewpoints. This is reflected in his College Application Wheel below.

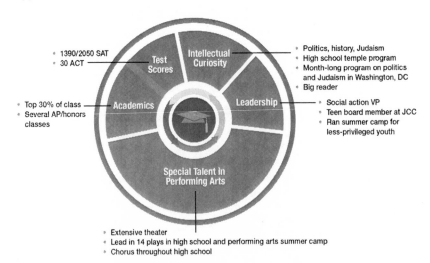

Noah's Application Wheel: Fall of Senior Year

- **Academics:** Noah took an academically rigorous curriculum with ten honors and/or AP classes, including AP US history, AP European history, AP English, and AP calculus AB. He has mostly A's with some B/B+'s.
- **Test scores:** On par with Noah's academic performance.
- **Extracurricular activities/special talents:** This was the largest piece of Noah's chart and for good reason. His passion for theater and performance was clear from his many leading roles.
- **Intellectual curiosity:** Noah pursued several varied but related academic interests at a high level outside of school. This category does not lend itself so easily to a resume listing. Noah had to demonstrate this slice of the pie chart in his personal statement on the application. His summer experience gave him an opportunity to reflect on his political views and how he approached forming opinions. It gave him a good experience to write about in his personal statement.
- **Leadership:** This piece of the chart was about equal in size to Noah's intellectual curiosity. He served in several leadership positions throughout his involvement in the Jewish Community Center. Noah had the opportunity to expand on his leadership skills and experiences during his summer through his involvement in the Panim el Panim program.
- **Athletics:** This was not a piece of Noah's wheel.
- **Other:** Noah was a legacy at the University of Pennsylvania and Brandeis University.
- **Financial:** Noah was a full-pay student.

Developing the College List

Noah wanted a school that appreciated his individual spirit while allowing him the flexibility to meld his multiple interests. Noah wanted a select college near a big city, with strong history and theater departments.

Key College Criteria for Noah

- Strong history and theater programs
- Located near a city
- Prestigious name
- Ability to participate actively in theater
- Decent Jewish population
- Intellectually curious students who don't take themselves too seriously

The Final List

The Reaches

- **University of Pennsylvania:** Penn may not have been the best fit, but he was a legacy.
- **Vassar College:** This is a selective liberal arts school with strong theater and history programs.

The Possibles

- **The College of William and Mary:** This was Noah's favorite school, a perfect blend of the three main things he wanted from a school: location, academics, and theater. Noah would increase his chances by applying early decision.
- **Tufts University:** Another school where he could be happy. Music is strong at Tufts, and Noah wanted to join an a capella group there. He considered it a strong second-choice school.

The Likelies

- **Brandeis University:** He was a legacy here as well. It is located near Boston and has strengths in his areas of interest.
- **Kenyon College:** While not necessarily near a big city, it is a select, academically challenging school with strong history and theater departments.
- **The College of New Jersey:** He viewed this as a strong state school with possible scholarship opportunities.

The Safety
- **Beloit College:** High possibility of merit scholarships and the overall feel of the school and majors were a good fit, even though it is not located near a big city.

Choosing an Essay Topic

After brainstorming with Noah about his strengths and interests, we identified several areas that he wanted to communicate within his application.

- Love for studying history
- Naturally self-motivated, independent, and intellectually curious
- Awareness of the world
- High-level thinking about world politics
- Acting and how that tied into his ability to see situations through different lenses

Narrowing Down Possible Topics

Experience: Noah's Major Experiences and Their Impacts
- **Participation in Panim el Panim** (cemented political interests). The program took him outside his comfort zone. Noah changed from this experience and began to see dialogue as a crucial part of politics.
- **Job at summer camp for refugee children** (learned to value his life circumstances). It was the first time he truly understood how much in his life he took for granted.
- **Attending performing arts sleep-away camp** (self-discovery and personal growth). In his hometown, Noah always felt a bit apart. He liked different music and films than his peers, and he often felt misunderstood. At his performing arts camp, Noah was able to connect with people and build confidence.

Issue: Personal, Local, National, or International Issue and Its Importance to Noah

- **Israeli-Palestinian conflict** (learned the importance of continually evolving personal opinions). While Noah was still developing his personal views on the topic, he strongly supported Israel. Because of that, he desired to learn more about the issue.

- **Frustration with the arrogance of modern political discourse** (aware of how it limits debates). Noah considered himself politically active and aware. From personal experience, he understood how all issues have complex sides and that there is validity to numerous viewpoints and opinions.

Person: Individuals Who Have Had a Significant Impact on Noah's Life and Outlook

- **Father** (imparted values and a sense of humor). While Noah's father had different interests than his son, he had always been supportive and shared with him his love of Woody Allen films.

- **The director of *The Provoked Wife*,** a play that Noah starred in at French Woods Festival summer camp (shared sense of humor and joy). He was one of the few people who truly shared and appreciated Noah's sense of humor. That director was one of the first adults in Noah's life who daily sought out his passions and made Noah relax and have fun.

- **Michael Moore** (source of political awakening). In seventh grade, Noah read Moore's book *Downsize This!* He found the book funny, informative, and eye-opening. That book started Noah on his journey to seek out further information. And after reading, he found himself paying greater attention to national and international issues.

■ ■ ■ Possible Essay Topic Summary Chart ■ ■ ■
Experience and Its Impact
Participation in Panim el Panim
Cemented political interests
Job at summer camp for refugee children
Learned to value his life circumstances
Attending performing arts sleep-away camp
Self-discovery and personal growth
Issue and Its Importance
Israeli-Palestinian conflict
Importance of continually developing personal opinions
Frustration with the arrogance of modern political discourse
Aware of how it limits debates
Person and His or Her Impact
Father
Imparted values and a sense of humor
Director of *The Provoked Wife*
First adult who shared his sense of humor
Michael Moore
Source of political awakening

The Personal Statement Essay

Noah decided to write about his summer experience and his political awakening because he felt his angle was his intellectual curiosity. Also, the story would provide pertinent examples of how Noah thought about and approached his passions and interests at a high level. These topics worked for the Common Application essay prompt "Discuss an accomplishment or event, formal or informal, that marked your transition from childhood to adulthood within your culture, community, or family." It would show

how he became an adult within his community by developing his own point of view rather than blindly following others' points of view.

Noah began the personal statement with a quote from a little-known historian about how lack of debate precipitated the Civil War.

> *Men ceased to discuss their problems, dropped the effort to compromise their differences…and resorted to the use of force.*
> **—Prof. Avery Craven**

He then described his hopes for his experience at a political-action-centered summer program in Washington, DC.

This past summer I spent four weeks in Washington, DC, which for me is like a toddler living in Disney World. The program was about Judaism, government, and community service. I came to the trip with an expectation that there would be great political discussions among people who were ideologically diverse and shared my passion for government. I could not wait to start slugging it out, politically.

Noah then recounted a time during the program when he understood firsthand the necessity of treating opposing political views with respect and consideration.

Within the first week it became clear that there was a disproportionately large liberal bias among the other people on the program. There were no more than five conservative kids on this program of sixty, and most of their ideas were easily disregarded or squelched. At one point on the trip I had said that I was not completely in favor of affirmative action. The negative reaction of the people I was talking to was so swift, it was like a giant cow brander seared my forehead with the word "conservative." Thankfully, I didn't have any other major ideological faux pas because I did not want to be permanently labeled with this word.

While Noah initially tried to hide his political views, he quickly realized that he was, in fact, much more open-minded than his peers on the trip.

The watershed moment of this trip came when an ultra-orthodox rabbi spoke to us about community organizing and civil disobedience. The rabbi made some statements about diluting the power of Jewish leadership groups. Immediately my peers, who, like me, had been weaned on Jewish Federations and community centers, were up in arms. Loud whispers circulated the room about how conservative he was and even his light-hearted comments were deemed offensive and outrageous. I was incensed. I found this rabbi quite liberal. He believed in intermarriage between Jews and non-Jews as well as the concept of secular Judaism. I was even more put off by the fact that a week earlier when Ruth Messinger, the head of American Jewish World Service, spoke to us, most people on the program lapped up her words like warm cream because of her history of liberalism.

Noah tied back to the opening quote.

Suddenly I recalled Professor Craven's quote. I had read this quote last year in AP US history in a packet of essays on the Civil War. This piece of text comes from an essay that contends that a breakdown of the democratic process is what truly caused the Civil War. Although it raised my eyebrows in a moment of ponderous thought, I simply dismissed it as the foolish rambling of a crackpot historian. This moment of recall made me realize that what he wrote is happening in our country right now. More and more people are not listening to each other when they speak about political issues.

He revealed that he too had been guilty of only listening to one point of view prior to this experience.

In hindsight, I can freely admit that prior to this experience, I was equally guilty of not listening to opinions different than my own. I first became intrigued in politics in 7th grade when I read Michael Moore's *Downsize This!* However, I was solely interested in liberal perspectives on issues, without ever pausing to heed the words of an Ann Coulter or a Sean Hannity on the conservative right. However, after this epiphany, I now take the time to listen to multiple opinions.

Noah took advantage of this essay to show at a high level his passion for history and politics, which seemingly runs counter to his strong theatrical resume. He closed the essay with a sense of humor to show his personality.

The message I took away from this experience is twofold. The first is that I need a college experience where people from across the political spectrum can speak freely. The second is that I need to start reading more crackpot theories.

The Short Answer

Some colleges ask students to write a short essay describing one of their activities in more detail. After using the personal statement essay to give an in-depth example of his intellectual curiosity, Noah used the short answer to discuss how his other passions—theater and performance—enriched his life. Noah avoided a simple essay about how theatrical performance increased his self-confidence. He stayed true to his voice and brought the short answer to a higher level by showing how he was changed as a person by a particular performance. Within the short answer, Noah also explained how his enthusiasm for understanding politics and history linked with his approach to understanding characters and their motivations.

Two summers ago I was cast as Sir John Brute, the lead in the Restoration comedy *The Provoked Wife*. My character's ideal day included using his verbal wit to irritate his wife, chasing around prostitutes (or as he endearingly called them his "cakes and pastries"), and drinking himself into a never-ending stupor. I wore a white wig, tights, a fat suit, cuffs, and an ascot. I felt the irreverence of this unseemly character rub off on me, but in a positive way. Before I played Sir John, I was constantly afraid of doing or saying something stupid. But after this role I no longer cared about sounding foolish. At the end of the show I was tired, sweaty, and thirsty, but I felt like I could go on all night because I was having so much fun.

Supplemental Essays by School

Many schools on the Common Application also require students to write supplemental essays specific for their school. The College of William and Mary has an optional essay (which most students choose to do) to write about anything they would like to round out their application. Noah struggled with what to write, as he wanted to show something different than his other two writing pieces. After much thought, he decided to write about why William and Mary was a great fit for him because he had compelling reasons for wanting to attend.

In his optional essay, Noah linked his love of dressing up in colonial garb to future opportunities to continue this quirky passion within the school community and surrounding area.

Where I grew up, I got strange looks for dressing in colonial clothing and talking like an Englishman. At William and Mary, not only would I fit in with the surroundings, I could probably get college credit for it.

Complementary Angles

Letters of Recommendation
- Noah had a good connection with his history teacher from his junior year and he knew that his history teacher was a strong writer.

- Noah also asked his science teacher for a letter because she was able to show another side of him as a student. Noah worked extremely hard in that class, even though it was not one of his strengths. The science teacher was able to speak to Noah's work ethic.

Brag Sheet/Resume

Noah included a detailed theatrical resume to highlight his time commitment and talent within his passion for theater.

Supplemental Materials

Noah assembled a five-minute DVD presenting highlights from his onstage performances. It used footage shot by his parents. This DVD was sent along to all schools where Noah applied. It provided a piece that could not be gleaned from an essay, recommendation, or resume listing.

Additional Information

Noah did not have any extenuating circumstances to report in his record. He uploaded his detailed brag sheet/resume here.

Results

Noah was accepted to William and Mary through early decision and did not need to apply to any other schools.

Final Decision

The College of William and Mary

What Can You Learn from Noah's Story?
Questions to Ask Yourself

- How can you use your summer(s) to either pursue one of your interests in more depth or round out your profile?
- What is your favorite subject in school? Have you done more research on it outside of school? Could you go deeper into one of your academic or personal interests? How? Can you create a

plan for yourself to go deeper either over the summer or during the school year?

- How do your interests match the school(s) to which you are applying?
- Why do you pursue the extracurricular activities that you do? What drives you to do it?
- What, if anything, is quirky about your personality? How can you incorporate that into your essays?

Notes

2

FEYDI
THE FIRST-GENERATION
NIGERIAN PRE-MED RUNNER

Lessons Learned during the Application Process

In this case, you will see how your family background can mold your personality and work ethic. Feydi's story will also demonstrate how she maintained two distinct personalities, a more open, playful one with her extended Nigerian family, and a more buttoned-up, formal one among her peers. She did this because she felt as though she had to both please her parents and represent her culture in a positive way to the outside world. You will see how she was able to use that to her advantage and secure a scholarship to a top school.

Feydi's Snapshot

- GPA: 4.2 (weighted, out of 4.3)
- Rigor: 12 AP/honors classes
- SAT: 1330/2030

- ACT with writing: N/A
- Class rank: top 10 percent

About Feydi

- Main interests: science, pre-med
- Feydi's parents were both born in Nigeria and came to the United States for college. She was the oldest of three girls and was very close with her family.
- She went to a suburban high school and was often the only African American student among her peers.
- She ran track throughout high school and enjoyed being able to find an identity for herself outside her family heritage and academic prowess.
- She participated in a mini medical program to gain exposure to medicine.
- She also helped her dad with a charity that he founded to provide health care in Nigeria.
- She had a large extended Nigerian family and community with whom she spent a lot of time. Her grandmother lived with her for many years.
- She had a strong financial need as the oldest of three girls with the intention of going to medical school after college.

Personality Profile

Feydi was an extremely focused, hardworking student. She took as many honors and AP classes as she could and put all her energy into doing well in school and getting good grades. She was often the only African American student in her honors and AP classes at her suburban high school. Given her cultural background, she had a very strong work ethic instilled in her by her parents, who came to the United States for college without knowing anyone. She also felt as if she had to set a good example for her younger siblings and meet her parents' expectations for success.

Her grandmother, with whom she was very close, lived with her family for many years. She went back to Nigeria for vacation, where she had a stroke and died due to insufficient medical care. Because of that, Feydi had her heart set on becoming a doctor and would do whatever she needed to fulfill this goal. Feydi ran track and applied a similar work ethic to improving her times. She also helped her father organize events for a foundation to raise money to start a school in Nigeria.

Creating Feydi's College Application Wheel

I met Feydi during the fall of her junior year. She was a strong, diligent student who knew that she wanted to be a doctor. We discussed the possibility of applying to some accelerated medical school programs and what that would entail. I encouraged her to look at going a more traditional route because I thought she could get into a college that was a better fit than some of the accelerated programs. Feydi also had a financial need since she was the oldest of three kids and wanted to go to medical school.

Since Feydi was interested in attending a highly selective college with the goal of becoming a doctor, we discussed ways she could show her intellectual curiosity in science by speaking with her teacher about some summer science opportunities or seeing if there was a science fair at her school. We also discussed applying for a mini medical program over the summer to gain exposure to the medical field in a deeper way. This would help her solidify her interest in medicine.

Academically, Feydi was a stellar student and her goal was to continue on this path. She decided to enroll in several AP classes her senior year, including biology, Spanish, European history, and calculus AB. This rigor would show her strength as a potential pre-med candidate. She also set a goal to reach 700+ in each section of the SAT to be competitive for the types of schools she wanted to attend.

Feydi ran for her high school's track team and was a member of the Spanish Club and Key Club. I suggested that she try to take on a leadership role in at least one of her activities since she had leadership potential and interest. Feydi loved running track and found the camaraderie and internal competition rewarding. She enjoyed her involvement in Key Club and having an outlet to help the community. She also spent a lot of time with her family and the extended Nigerian community.

Feydi's Strengths

- Strong, well-rounded student
- Hardworking and motivated
- High grades in challenging curriculum
- Accomplished athlete
- Burgeoning leadership skills and involvement in community service
- Multicultural background
- Underrepresented minority

Feydi's Weaknesses

- Intellectual curiosity and interest in medicine or science limited to classroom
- Had financial need
- Could increase leadership profile
- Test scores

Feydi's Checklist

Feydi had a strong academic record. Her goal was to continue with a rigorous curriculum particularly in math and science to show her potential as a pre-med candidate. She had to apply her strong work ethic to studying for the SAT to reach her goal of 700+ on each section.

Feydi needed to boost her intellectual curiosity in science, and I suggested that she attend a mini medical summer program and take an AP science her senior year. I also recommended that she continue with track and try to become a leader in one of her activities to put her in a good position for merit scholarships. Her family needed to determine their budget for college and make sure that Feydi knew what to expect.

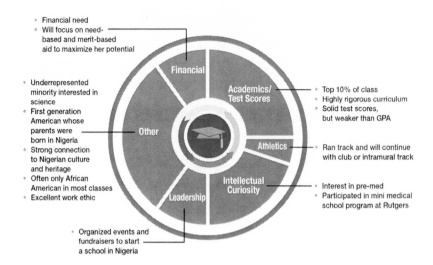

* Financial need
* Will focus on need-based and merit-based aid to maximize her potential

* Underrepresented minority interested in science
* First generation American whose parents were born in Nigeria
* Strong connection to Nigerian culture and heritage
* Often only African American in most classes
* Excellent work ethic

* Top 10% of class
* Highly rigorous curriculum
* Solid test scores, but weaker than GPA

* Ran track and will continue with club or intramural track

* Interest in pre-med
* Participated in mini medical school program at Rutgers

* Organized events and fundraisers to start a school in Nigeria

Feydi's Application Wheel: Fall of Senior Year

- **Academics:** Feydi had a strong academic record across the board. She needed to continue to push herself by taking AP classes in a variety of subjects, particularly in math and science.
- **Test scores:** Feydi's test scores were below her goal, particularly in math and critical reading. She had a 620 in critical reading and 570 in math at the end of her junior year; she reached 700 in the writing section. She had to study hard and do a lot of practice tests to bring up her scores to what she had originally hoped. Feydi took the test one more time in October and was able to bring up her scores closer to her goal, with a score of 1330 in critical reading and math and 2030 including writing.
- **Athletics:** Feydi enjoyed pushing herself in track. She found that this is one area where she did not have any outside pressure other than her own desire to succeed.
- **Special talent:** This was not a piece of Feydi's chart.
- **Intellectual curiosity:** Feydi got accepted into the mini medical school program at Rutgers Robert Wood Johnson Medical

School; this gave her the additional exposure to the medical field that she needed.

- **Leadership:** Feydi took on a leadership role in her father's nonprofit that raised money to start a school in Nigeria. She organized events and raised money. This combined her interest in helping others, leadership, and multicultural background.
- **Other:** Feydi's parents came from Nigeria to the United States for college, so she was a first-generation American. She was also an African American girl interested in science. Her strong sense of family and connection to her heritage represented another point of differentiation.
- **Financial:** Feydi needed to get substantial money to go to school. She focused on need-based aid as well as merit-based aid to maximize her potential.

Developing the College List

At first Feydi wanted to look at accelerated BAMD programs as well as select colleges with a strong science and pre-med curriculum. Once Feydi realized that her SAT scores were not high enough for her to compete in these programs, we changed strategies and focused only on colleges with strong science and pre-med programs and financial aid. She wanted a suburban campus with access to a city within four to five hours of her home in New Jersey. She also wanted a school that put a lot of emphasis on community service and whose students were accepting of a variety of cultures.

Key College Criteria for Feydi
- Open to any size school as long as it met her needs
- Preferred a suburban campus near a big city or a town
- Wanted to study science and be on a pre-med track
- Name of the school was very important
- Financial aid would play a significant role
- Opportunities to play intramural sports and be involved in community service

- Not interested in Greek life, but would like it if the school had good sports team and school spirit
- A preppy, liberal, down-to-earth student body

The Final List

The Reaches
- **University of Pennsylvania:** Penn has a great reputation and she fell in love with the campus and vibe of the school when she ran the Penn Relays with her track team.
- **Princeton University:** Princeton has an outstanding reputation, prestige, and good science programs. Feydi liked that it was close to home and has a beautiful campus.

The Possibles
- **Boston College:** Feydi loved the Jesuit philosophy of BC and felt very comfortable on campus. It also has a strong pre-med program.
- **Tufts University:** Feydi loved the feel of Tufts, but it did not offer any merit-based aid, so she had to see what sort of need-based aid came through. Her SATs were also on the low side for Tufts.
- **Villanova University:** Since Feydi liked BC so much, we added Villanova because it offers a Presidential Scholarship that covers all expenses. Villanova itself was a likely school, but it became a possible school taking into consideration the need for a Presidential Scholarship.

The Likelies
- **Boston University:** She liked the feel of BU, even though it is urban. It was on the original BAMD list for its seven-year medical school program, but she wanted to keep it on the current list for its good pre-med program and location.
- **University of Maryland at College Park:** Feydi liked the feel of UMD and knew that it would provide her with good science

classes, sports, and clubs. We were also fairly certain she would get into its scholars program and possibly get some money.

- **The College of New Jersey:** TCNJ has excellent science and pre-med programs and offers generous merit scholarships.

The Safeties

- **Rutgers:** Feydi liked the diversity of the student body and knew she would qualify for a scholarship.
- **Ursinus College:** Feydi knew she would get substantial merit money from Ursinus, and it has a great pre-med/science program.

Choosing an Essay Topic

After brainstorming with Feydi about her strengths and interests, we identified several areas that she wanted to communicate within her application.

- Her culture had influenced every part of her life and made her highly motivated, not for money or prestige, but to help others.
- She had a true passion for her culture and medicine and would share that passion with others.
- She was genuinely interested in biology, in particular how it has helped the human race evolve.
- Her grandmother taught her to learn from her mistakes and not dwell on them; this propelled her to work hard and always try to improve.

Narrowing Down Possible Topics

Experience: Feydi's Major Experiences and Their Impacts

- **Nigerian background** (instilled in her a sense of determination and desire to achieve at a high level). Feydi's grandmother lived with her for most of her childhood and teen years. Having the benefit of a multicultural and multigenerational upbringing gave Feydi a strong sense of her heritage; however, she was also the first one in her family to grow up in the United States. As a result, Feydi had to figure out everything herself. She often served as the liaison between cultures. She also felt like she had two different personas, one the dutiful oldest daughter of immigrants and the other a typical American high-achieving student. She never complained about the dichotomy in her background, but just accepted it all with a positive determination that came to represent her personality.

- **Winning the Paul Robeson Youth Achievement Award in middle school** (validated all her hard work). Feydi was one of three African American students in her high school, so when she won this award it was extremely powerful. She always felt like she had to work harder than anyone else to prove that she was just as intelligent as her white classmates. She never felt like she was treated any differently because of the color of her skin; however, internally she always felt like she was different because her parents did not grow up in the United States. This award validated all of her hard work, and she was extremely proud that she received it.

- **Track team.** Feydi found her home on the track team because it was the one place where she achieved only for herself. She could succeed through sheer determination, hard work, and talent.

Issue: Personal, Local, National, or International Issue and Its Importance to Feydi

- **Immigration.** Feydi felt strongly that new immigrants should not be allowed to become citizens unless they went through the same process as her parents and family did. She saw how hard her parents worked and was proud of their accomplishments.

Person: Individuals Who Have Had a Significant Impact on Feydi's Life and Outlook

- **Dad** (showed her how to effect change). Feydi's dad was part of an organization that started a school in Nigeria. Her family always held parties and fund-raisers for this school. When she visited the school one summer in Nigeria, she was able to see how difficult life is there. It made her even more grateful for the opportunities that she has in America and motivated her to do more. She wanted to become a doctor to go back to Nigeria and start a clinic to provide primary care to patients in Nigeria. Seeing how her family had been able to build a school and impact lives in their home country influenced her decision to go into medicine because that is where she felt she could have the most impact.

- **Uncles** (taught her about her culture). Her uncles lived with her when she was younger and instilled in her a sense of pride for her Nigerian culture. They also exposed her to different types of food.

■ ■ ■ Possible Essay Topic Summary Chart ■ ■ ■

Experience and Its Impact
Nigerian background
Instilled pride as well as a strong work ethic, motivation, and desire to prove her intellect
Winning the Paul Robeson Award
Validated her hard work and helped her see herself as equal to her peers despite her parents' immigrant background
Participation in track
Found a place to be herself and apply her strong work ethic
Issue and Its Importance
Immigration
This issue was close to her heart as she has seen her family immigrate through the proper channels and felt everyone else should

Person and His or Her Impact
Dad
Modeled how to effect change in the world through his participation in an organization that builds schools in Nigeria; helped her understand that medicine was where she could make her mark
Grandma
Taught her that failure was a natural part of life and not to be stymied by it
Uncles
Instilled a sense of pride in her background and exposed her to new foods

The Personal Statement Essay

Feydi wanted to show how she juggled two different sides of her personality: the one that she portrayed to her peers and the one that she showed to her family. However, she had found one place where those two sides could come together and thrive, on the track.

> In my life I feel like I maintain two distinct personas, a public and a private one. As the daughter of Nigerian immigrants, I have felt the need to create a public reputation of being studious, responsible, and determined… In private, I am more energetic and open. I have nothing to prove with my family because they love me unconditionally.
>
> Track and field is one area where these two diverse personalities fuse together. My public and personal personas disappear whenever I step onto the track because there I am only proving something to myself.

Feydi described how she put her hard work and determination to secure the coveted fourth position of the 4×400 meter relay team.

I was the first one on the track for practice and the last one to leave. I helped lead stretches, which showed my coach that I could be a leader while also cooperating with others. I ran while I was at home with the help of my dad and ran my hardest during practices.

This topic addressed the prompt "Describe a place or environment where you are perfectly content. What do you do or experience there, and why is it meaningful to you?" She was able to show why track made her content and was meaningful to her.

Track requires more than just bookwork and letter grades. It tests my endurance, my strength, my speed, and my team dynamic. In track, I found an outlet, a place where I had balance; a place where I did not need to impress people at school or follow the Nigerian traditions. I found a place where I could strive because of my own personal talents. When I am on the track, I have no boundaries, troubles, or woes.

Feydi was able to weave a compelling story that showed the reader what drives her and how she will bring these conflicting yet powerful motivating factors to everything that she does.

The Short Answer

While Feydi alluded to her Nigerian background in her main personal statement, she wanted to give some context for her interest in becoming a doctor. She chose to write her short answer about helping her dad raise money to build a school in Nigeria. The risk in choosing this topic was that the organization was her dad's activity, not her own. Therefore she focused on how her involvement in this program gave her exposure to life in Nigeria and motivated her to find her own way to make a difference.

These pictures inspired me to continue to assist my dad but to also find ways that I could help people in my own way. I found this solution in my love for the sciences and the medical field. One day I hope to return to Nigeria as a certified physician to start a health clinic so that people can receive basic health needs. I feel that helping people that are ill and assisting them in living normal lives would give me a purpose in life.

Supplemental Essays by School

Feydi had several supplemental essays to write for her list of schools. They fell into six different categories:

1. Why this school? (Penn, Tufts, BU)
2. Describe a time when you have been transformed. (Villanova, Penn [optional])
3. What is your academic interest and how can it be met at this school? (Penn, BU, University of Maryland)
4. How has your family background influenced your life/person of influence? (Tufts, Princeton)
5. How has diversity played a role in your life? (Villanova Presidential Scholarship essay)

Why This School?

This essay required that Feydi be very specific about the qualities of each school that fit with her personality. She described her personal experience visiting each school and how the pre-med curriculum and activities fit with how she wanted to study and learn. She gave examples of clubs that she would join, classes she would take, and places she would go specific to each school's offerings.

Describe a Time You Have Been Transformed

This was the prompt for Villanova University, but she was also able to use a variation of the same essay for one of Penn's optional essays.

She described her experience attending the National Young Leaders Conference as a shy freshman. She described a leadership exercise that shaped the group and herself.

> On the first evening, all the groups were assembled in the conference hall for an activity called the human knot; it became a kind of competition to see which group was the best. At this point we were all still getting to know each other. Since the program was meant for leaders, we ran into the problem of everyone wanting to take the lead. We tangled our arms into a huge mass of flesh and attempted to remove ourselves from the knot but to no avail. To our dismay, we were one of the last groups to finish. On the last day of the conference, we tried the exercise again to see if our communication and cooperation skills had improved. To our surprise and joy, we were the first group to untangle ourselves. As soon as we jumbled our arms together, each person took charge of a different step. One person untangled another and then another person took charge of untangling the next and this process worked until we were all separated.

Feydi began the program apprehensive, but emerged with confidence and a new perspective on leadership. This was a great essay to use for Penn as well because it showed her leadership skills in a concrete way.

Academic Interests

Feydi used these essays to talk about her interest in biology and how she wanted to become a doctor. She pulled out specific course and research opportunities at each school that would help her fulfill her goals.

Family Background/Person of Influence

She wrote two variations of this essay, but focused on how her mother's unwavering support and belief in her pushed her never to give up.

She described an example of how she struggled to memorize material in a summer medical school program and how her mom encouraged her to keep trying until she mastered it. She wrote a longer version of this for Princeton's question about a person who influenced you and why.

Role of Diversity

This question was for the Villanova Presidential Scholarship. While Feydi was certainly a minority, she had never really felt discriminated against because of her skin color or heritage. Instead, her internal feeling of being different drove her to achieve even more and positively represent her race and her culture.

> This has always been an internal conflict that nobody ever really understood. For one, I desired to show my classmates the true meaning of what it was to be a Nigerian. Many of my friends did not know a lot about foreign countries. So I felt that I could be a representative for my home country. I wanted to show that all African nations were not third world countries filled with uneducated individuals. A lot of motivated, hardworking people, such as my parents, emerged from these countries and I was a product of this. I set this lofty goal for myself and in my opinion I accomplished it. I am the only African American girl in the honors/AP program at my school and I have been appointed to leadership positions in my extracurricular activities. I have tamed my internal beasts, but they will never completely diminish because they drive me to succeed.

She continued to talk about how she hopes to become a leader in a multicultural awareness group at Villanova since it was not a hugely diverse community.

Complementary Angles

Letters of Recommendation

- Feydi got letters of recommendation from her AP biology teacher and her Spanish teacher. Both knew her well and could speak to her strong work ethic.
- She also got a letter of recommendation from her track coach, who could show how hard she worked for the team.

Brag Sheet/Resume

- Feydi's resume emphasized her involvement on her track team, the cultural awareness club, and all of the health care–related programs that she attended.
- It also highlighted her many leadership experiences and awards from school.

Supplemental Materials

- Feydi had no supplemental materials; however, she did have to interview for the Villanova Presidential Scholarship. She did not make the first twelve finalists, but thankfully somebody dropped out and she was next in line. We did a mock interview to get her comfortable speaking about herself.

Additional Information

- Feydi did not have any extenuating circumstances to report in her record. She uploaded her detailed resume here.

Results

The Reaches

- **University of Pennsylvania:** Accepted ($30,000 need-based financial aid)
- **Princeton University:** Denied

The Possibles
- **Boston College:** Accepted
- **Tufts University:** Accepted
- **Villanova University:** Accepted (received Presidential Scholarship including tuition, room, board, and books)

The Likelies
- **Boston University:** Accepted ($30,000 financial aid)
- **University of Maryland at College Park:** Accepted into honors program
- **The College of New Jersey:** Accepted ($10,000 merit aid)

The Safeties
- **Rutgers:** Accepted (full-tuition scholarship)
- **Ursinus College:** Accepted (nominated for a $27,000 merit scholarship, but declined)

Final Decision
Villanova University (a free ride at a great school was hard to pass up).

What Can You Learn from Feydi's Story?
Questions to Ask Yourself
- What drives you to succeed? Is it your family background? Fear of seeming inferior? How can you share that story with colleges?
- How has your cultural background influenced your life?
- What are your personal life goals? How can you tie that into a potential career?
- When do you feel like you can be yourself? How does that drive the decisions that you make?
- How can you use your family background to show how you will contribute to a college community?

Notes

3

KYLE
THE ATHLETE
TURNED ACTOR

Lessons Learned during the Application Process

In this case, you will realize that failure and regret can be great drivers for success. Kyle's story shows how his fear of taking his rightful position as a member of the varsity soccer team led to regret. Instead of wallowing in his regret, he used it to fuel his desire to become an actor. He shows how past failure can lead to future success.

Kyle's Snapshot

- GPA: 3.86 (weighted, out of 4.3)
- Rigor: 6 AP/honors classes
- SAT: 1060/1600
- ACT with writing: NA
- Class rank: top 25 percent

About Kyle

- Main interests: theater, film, communications
- Kyle lacked confidence, but through acting and increased self-insight, his confidence grew.
- He was a strong athlete, but changed focus from soccer to acting during his junior year; however, he wanted to continue playing club soccer in school.
- Kyle had intellectual curiosity for film; he applied what he learned in English to analyze books to analyze films.
- He wanted to be close to New York City to go on auditions.
- He was politically conservative.
- Kyle had financial need because he had a twin brother who was also going to college.

Personality Profile

Kyle had spent most of his life until the end of his sophomore year playing soccer. He was a highly talented soccer player, but got psyched out when he made the varsity team as a sophomore and other players in his class resented him for it. He pulled back from the varsity team and stayed on junior varsity because he was not confident enough to ignore his teammates. That year, the varsity team won the state finals, and Kyle always regretted his decision.

During sophomore year, Kyle started taking acting classes outside of school. He had never pursued acting before, but with his good looks and natural abilities, he quickly rose to the top of his class. He secured an agent and built his confidence. Kyle was quiet by nature and understated his talents. His success in acting brought him out of his shell and exposed him to a new world outside of soccer. He wanted to continue acting during college and had a long-term goal of owning a talent agency. He wanted to study theater or film in college, but he also wanted the opportunity to study business or communications because he did not feel confident enough that he would make a living in the entertainment industry. He also had a strong intellectual curiosity in analyzing film.

Creating Kyle's College Application Wheel

I met Kyle in February of his junior year. I learned that he was an excellent soccer player and had been pursuing soccer almost exclusively until his sophomore year, when he caught the acting bug. He started taking acting classes at an acting studio near his home and had gone out on several auditions for commercials and modeling. He went to a large, diverse suburban high school. He was hardworking and focused on school, and he had done well in a moderately challenging curriculum. He lacked confidence, but it was clear that he had a lot of emerging talents in acting and that he was an excellent student with a keen analytical mind. In the right environment, he would thrive. He also had a twin brother whom I did not meet but who was interested in going to Rutgers.

We identified that Kyle was a good student, but that he was not challenging himself enough academically and should pursue a more rigorous curriculum during his senior year. He also needed to increase his test scores, if possible, into the 600+ range for each section of the SAT to match his high GPA. Since Kyle's family would have two kids in school at the same time, financial aid—particularly merit aid—would factor significantly into his list of schools.

I asked Kyle about his switch from soccer player to actor. He told me that he started taking acting classes outside of school and realized that he had a talent for it. He still enjoyed soccer but wanted to broaden his experience. His good looks and athletic build made him attractive to an agent. He had entered many talent showcases through his acting studio. We discussed continuing with his passion for acting, but also the need to push his GPA up closer to a 4.0 and increase his test scores to make him eligible for merit aid.

Kyle regularly attended church and had a strong sense of spirituality from his participation in church-related activities; however, he did not do much community service. I suggested that he get more involved with his church through volunteering and community service.

Kyle's Strengths
- Acting talent
- Athletic talent
- Hardworking
- Strong grades in challenging curriculum
- Clear future goals

Kyle's Weaknesses
- Test scores were weaker than grades
- Could increase the rigor of his curriculum
- Limited community service

Kyle's Checklist

Kyle had a strong academic record. His goal was to continue pushing himself academically and try to nudge his junior year grades up slightly to mostly A's. Kyle needed to show that he was challenging himself more during his senior year by taking AP psychology (an area of interest to him), honors physics, honors English, and honors global studies, in addition to calculus and Spanish 4. This would signal to colleges that Kyle was academically prepared and motivated and a good candidate for merit money.

Kyle needed study more to improve his SATs to match his high GPA. If he were unable to raise his scores, then we would focus our search on test-optional schools to give him the best chance of being eligible for merit aid. I suggested that he should also continue pursuing his acting talents along with his soccer, because it would show that he can contribute in multiple ways to a prospective college. Many schools also offer merit aid for students with a special talent. Finally, Kyle needed to find some additional ways to be active in his community through his church or the YMCA.

Kyle continued to pursue his acting studies and went on to receive several awards and kudos from his acting school. He also took a more rigorous academic program while continuing to play varsity soccer. The combination of pushing himself academically, theatrically, and athletically and the success that followed boosted Kyle's confidence, which we were able to reflect in his application. He also became a camp counselor at the YMCA for fourth to seventh grade boys, as well as helped senior citizens through his church.

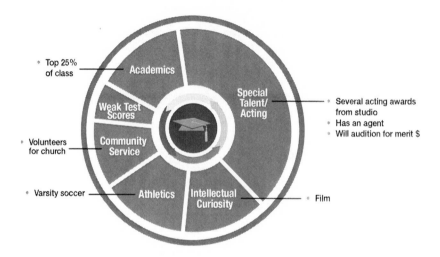

Kyle's Application Wheel: Fall of Senior Year

- **Academics:** Kyle had a strong GPA, and with a more rigorous senior year schedule, he showed that he was ready for the challenge of college.

- **Test scores:** Kyle's test scores were below his academic performance. He needed to improve these or focus on test-optional schools.

- **Athletics:** Kyle had a long history with soccer and received two varsity letters in high school. He learned a lesson about letting others define what you will do by not playing varsity soccer his sophomore year. He would continue to play intramural sports in college.

- **Special talent:** This was another large piece of Kyle's chart and shows that he was multifaceted. His relatively new but strong acting component balanced out his previous success in soccer. It also made for an interesting story about refocusing his passion and taking a risk in a new area.

- **Intellectual curiosity:** Kyle showed this through his commitment to acting, analysis of film, and understanding of the talent industry. He pushed beyond his comfort zone and pursued a totally new area. He also showed this through challenging himself more during his senior year.
- **Leadership:** Kyle did not have a huge leadership piece of the pie, but that developed as his confidence continued to grow stronger. He also took on some leadership through being a counselor at the YMCA over the summer.
- **Other:** Kyle had an agent and auditioned for several modeling and acting roles. This foray into professional acting set him apart.
- **Financial:** Kyle needed to get merit aid to bring the cost of any school he attends on par with in-state options such as Rutgers.

Developing the College List

Kyle wanted a small liberal arts college with a strong theater and film program. He also wanted to study business or communications as a second major or minor. He wanted a school that would be close to New York City so that he could continue to go on auditions, but he also wanted there to be a lot of opportunity to perform on campus. Kyle also needed financial aid or merit aid to bring the cost down to the price of Rutgers.

Key College Criteria for Kyle
- Small liberal arts college with good faculty interaction
- Located within 1–1.5 hours of New York City or Boston to facilitate going on auditions
- Wanted to study film, theater, and possibly business
- Name of the school was not as important as the fit
- Needed financial aid or merit aid
- Wanted to learn to think critically
- Some sports presence would be nice

The Final List

The Reaches
Kyle did not want to apply to any reaches because he knew he would not likely get any merit aid at a reach school. His reach schools would have been Tisch School of the Arts at New York University and Connecticut College.

The Possibles
- **Muhlenberg College:** This was Kyle's favorite school. He felt very comfortable with the student body when he visited. It has academic strengths in film, theater, and business, and they offer generous merit-based aid. It is a bit far from New York City, but there are lots of opportunities to perform on campus. It is also test-optional.

The Likelies
- **Ursinus College:** Ursinus is a strong liberal arts college with theater and business programs. It is close to New York City, but Philadelphia is also emerging as a location for filming due to lower costs.
- **Rutgers:** This was a good financial safety school for Kyle, and while not a small school, the highly selective theater department at the Mason Gross School of the Arts is much smaller, and he could take classes in business. His twin brother was going there.
- **Quinnipiac University:** Kyle felt comfortable with the student body here.

The Safety
- **Ramapo College:** This was Kyle's financial safety school, since it is a New Jersey state school.

Choosing an Essay Topic

After brainstorming with Kyle about his strengths and interests, we identified several areas that he wanted to communicate within his application.

- Regret as a powerful motivator
- His ability to transform from an insecure soccer player to a confident actor
- His strong sense of faith and desire to help others
- His journey to self-discovery through acting and soccer

Narrowing Down Possible Topics

Experience: Kyle's Major Experiences and Their Impacts

- **Playing competitive soccer** (taught him downside of fear). Kyle played competitive soccer from a very young age. He had a natural talent for soccer, but the pressure and the verbal abuse from coaches stripped his confidence when he was younger. He ultimately developed a thick skin, but at times he wondered if the pressure was worth it. He also regretted not staying on the varsity soccer team during his sophomore year because that year they won the state championship.
- **Acting** (learned to push through the fear). He did not want to let the regret he felt from shying away from soccer stay with him, so in acting he pushed himself out of his comfort zone, past the fear, and ultimately succeeded. It was a great outlet for him to build confidence.

Issue: Personal, Local, National, or International Issue and Its Importance to Kyle

- **Youth sports** (thinking about how to change his experience for next generation). He wondered how to teach competition without stripping confidence for younger participants.

Person: Individuals Who Have Had a
Significant Impact on Kyle's Life and Outlook

- **Mom** (wanted a more financially secure life than her). Kyle saw his mom working very hard as freelance marketer without a steady paycheck. He wanted to have a more financially stable career and was focused on achieving that.

- **Chris Gardner from the movie** *The Pursuit of Happyness* (showed him how to pursue a goal doggedly). He saw how hard Chris Gardner worked toward his goal and never gave up regardless of the circumstances. He motivated Kyle to continue to pursue his dreams even if it was difficult. Kyle modeled his life and work ethic after Gardner's.

■ ■ ■ Possible Essay Topic Summary Chart ■ ■ ■

Experience and Its Impact

Participation in competitive soccer
Developed a thick skin and realized that fear and regret will not get him to success

Acting
Learned to push beyond fear and develop self-confidence

Issue and Its Importance

Youth sports
Importance of teaching competition without stripping confidence

Person and His or Her Impact

Mother
Wanted to create a more financially stable career based on how hard he saw her work

Chris Gardner
Desired to emulate his hard work and perseverance in the face of challenges to follow a dream

The Personal Statement Essay

Kyle decided to write about his journey toward overcoming fear by describing how he let fear keep him from playing varsity soccer as a sophomore and that he regretted that decision terribly. When he switched gears toward acting, his regret fueled his desire to push through his fear. This topic answered the Common Application essay prompt "Recount an incident or time when you experienced failure. How did it affect you, and what lessons did you learn?"

He was also motivated by the movie *The Pursuit of Happyness* because Chris Gardner showed him how he could push through anything with hard work and persistence. He started his essay with a quote from the movie.

> *You got a dream, you gotta protect it. People can't do something themselves, they wanna tell you that you can't do it. You want something? Go get it.*
> —**Chris Gardner**, *The Pursuit of Happyness*

He tied that quote into his experience with soccer.

Soccer was always a big part of my life. Scratch that—it was the only thing in my life. My schedule on a normal high school day included school, soccer, homework, sleep, school, soccer, homework, sleep, and so on. As a sophomore, the varsity coach saw something in me during tryouts. However, the other players told me that I couldn't play varsity as a sophomore. The sad part is I believed them. I took myself out of contention to make the varsity squad because of the pressure. That year the varsity team won the state championship and was named one of the top 25 high school teams in the country. Sitting in the stands at the College of New Jersey, celebrating with the kids who told me I couldn't be on that field while the team I should have been on is getting its name printed in history, I felt ashamed of myself.

Kyle regretted his decision terribly; he felt he had failed.

During his junior year, he found an ad for an acting class. He wrote about his initial hesitation and linked it to his soccer failure.

I had always wanted to pursue acting, but I never did because I let other people's opinions and lack of confidence in me dictate my actions. But after the soccer experience, I realized that I can't live my life based on what others think about me and I auditioned for an acting school. The manager told me to do a commercial for her and she goes, "You're in." At that moment I froze. Pressure started to build as I thought about possible rejection from others rather than my own goals. Before I told her yes I went outside and sat in the car. I did not want to say to myself in twenty years, "What could have been?" So I walked back in and signed up and decided to let my talent, my training, and my drive decide what kind of actor I would become one day.

He signed up, and it was in acting that Kyle found his passion. He also realized that if this was his dream, then, just like Chris Gardner, he had to push through the fear and do things outside of his comfort zone.

Now I have a dream to own a talent agency, and I have to protect it by building a shield, blocking out people telling me I don't have the look or the experience. Acting has forced me to overcome my shyness and do things that I don't necessarily want to do. I am more comfortable presenting in front of the class and speaking with my fellow classmates. I've learned how to calm my nerves on set, so now I no longer rely on other people's judgment to determine who I am or what I can be.

Kyle showed how he grew as a person and realized that no matter what life brings him, he would work through his fear to succeed. He continued to reference the original quote of following and protecting his dream of becoming an actor or talent agent.

The Short Answer

He used this for schools that asked the student to describe an activity in more detail. After using the personal statement essay to give an in-depth description of how Kyle successfully changed his ambition from soccer to acting, he decided to focus his short answer on his love of helping others. He continued with the theme of following his dreams, but this time his dream was to help others.

> At my church, my favorite activity was visiting Runnel's Senior Citizen Hospital every year around Christmastime. I imagined each patient as my grandparents. I always did whatever I could to help them and it gave me comfort in knowing that I could be a substitute grandchild for these people for a short time. Whenever they smile or say thank you, I know that at that moment, I performed a good deed. By being able to give back to these people in need, I feel like my dreams are not really dreams anymore. Instead, I am making them a reality.

Supplemental Essays by School

None of Kyle's schools required a supplemental essay.

Complementary Angles

Letters of Recommendation
- Kyle asked his math and English teachers for letters of recommendation because they would show different sides of his academic strengths.
- Kyle also got supplementary letters of recommendation from his acting coach and his soccer coach. Each of them was able to present a different aspect of Kyle's personality and strengths.

Brag Sheet/Resume
- Kyle broke his brag sheet into three distinct categories of excellence: soccer, acting, and community service. In his main

personal statement and short answer, he discussed the "why" for these activities, and the brag sheet was able to showcase the extent of his activities in more detail.

Supplemental Materials/Audition

- Kyle auditioned for Muhlenberg College to demonstrate his acting talent and to be eligible for a talent-based grant.
- Had he wanted to pursue soccer further, he would have sent an athletic resume to the coach, but he decided to focus on acting while in college.

Additional Information

- Kyle did not have any extenuating circumstances to report in his record. He uploaded his detailed brag sheet/resume here.

Results

Kyle was accepted to all the schools to which he applied. However, after visiting Muhlenberg, he decided that it was his clear first choice. Muhlenberg has a late early decision deadline of February 1, and he spoke with someone from the admissions department who advised him that Muhlenberg gives out more money to early decision candidates. So, he changed his application status from regular decision to early decision in January. As a result, he received a substantial financial and merit aid package, which made Muhlenberg affordable.

Final Decision

Muhlenberg College

What Can You Learn from Kyle's Story?
Questions to Ask Yourself

- What is something that you regret? Why? What did you learn from this experience? How have you grown as a result of that experience?

- What are your passions outside of school? How are you pursuing them?
- What risks have you taken in your life? How did they turn out for you? If you had the chance to do them again, would you? Why or why not?
- What talent(s) do you have that can help you receive some merit aid?
- What is your budget for college? How can you approach the process in a financially strategic way?

Notes

HAYLEY
THE RELUCTANT ENGINEER
AND RUNNER

Lessons Learned during the Application Process

In this case, you will see how Hayley grew as a person by applying lessons learned in running cross-country and track to her academics. You will also see how she was able to combine two seemingly disconnected interests (Model UN and strength in math and science) to create a unique angle as a girl interested in engineering. Hayley's story also shows the benefit of doing a lot of research in a given area of interest before determining her major (or at least before writing about why a particular area interested her at a given school).

Hayley's Snapshot

- GPA: 4.01 (weighted, out of 4.36)
- Rigor: 11 AP/honors classes
- SAT: 1480/2280

- ACT with writing: 24
- Class rank: top 20 percent

About Hayley

- Main interests: business, math, science
- Hayley was a well-rounded student who was not entirely sure what she wanted to study in school at the beginning of the process.
- She ran track and cross-country throughout high school and enjoyed the camaraderie of the team and the ability to see herself improve through hard work.
- She participated in Model UN and enjoyed debating with peers about various issues.
- She was open to the location of the school and wanted a medium to large school with a lot of opportunities.
- She was also involved in the Jewish community through her summer camp and a community service program at the Jewish Community Center.
- She did not have a strong financial need, but her older sister was in college at the University of Texas, so finances did play some role.

Personality Profile

Hayley was a strong student and did particularly well in math and science. She took a balanced course load, pushing herself in math, science, and Spanish. She challenged herself by taking honors or AP classes in her areas of strength and took academic-level classes in history and English. This gave her the opportunity to work hard but not burn out.

This balance extended to her extracurricular activities. Hayley joined the track and cross-country teams during her freshman year and continued to run throughout high school. She also participated in Model UN, taking on some leadership as a subcommittee co-chair. During her junior year, she began volunteering at the Jewish Community Center. She continued to do well in school and was nominated by her teachers to be a transition leader during her senior year to help freshmen transition into high school.

Creating Hayley's College Application Wheel

I met Hayley in January of her sophomore year. She was a strong student and had an interest in math and science. At that point, she did not know what she wanted to study in college, which is typical of most sophomores. I suggested that she participate in a pre-college program the following summer between her junior and senior years that would expose her to engineering or a deeper level of science to help her home in on her academic interests. We also identified that she should pursue at least three AP classes in math and science during her senior year.

Since Hayley felt more comfortable with math and science, she did not typically read for pleasure. I suggested that she try to find books of interest to increase her vocabulary through reading, as well as visit the website freerice.com for five minutes per day to increase her vocabulary. We set a goal for 1350/2050 for her SATs or 29–31 on her ACTs with writing to match her current GPA.

Hayley was involved in Model UN, cross-country, and track, but was considering trying out for volleyball her junior year. I asked her if she had an interest or aptitude to become a leader in one of her activities. She was not sure, but she wanted to give it a go, so we set a goal for her to run for a leadership position with Model UN for the next year. We also decided that she could try out for volleyball the following year, but if she did not make it, to stick with cross-country and track and think about becoming captain by senior year.

Finally, we talked about areas where she could get involved in the community because she had very little community service. Since she had a connection with the Jewish community through her camp and temple, she decided to get involved in a new Teen Action Service Corps (TASC) program at the Jewish Community Center that combined leadership and community service. I also suggested that she look into becoming a transition leader at her high school to help freshmen acclimate.

Hayley's Strengths

- Math and science
- Hardworking
- Strong grades in challenging curriculum
- Desire to push herself if given a plan

Hayley's Weaknesses

- Limited community service
- Did a lot of things, but no clear focus or depth
- Limited leadership

Hayley's Checklist

Hayley had a strong academic record. Her goal was to continue with a rigorous curriculum, particularly in math and science, where she had an aptitude and interest. I suggested that it would be great if Hayley could find a passion for one of these subjects, rather than just doing it because it comes easily for her.

Hayley needed to work on her community service and leadership. Since she had a strong connection to her Jewish background, she decided to get more involved in TASC and also participate in a program that pairs

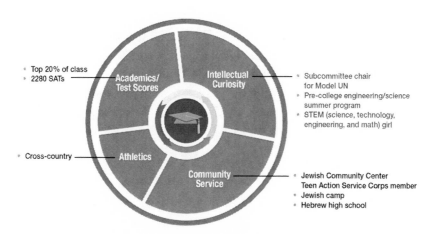

Hayley's Application Wheel: Fall of Senior Year

Jewish teens with teens in a neighboring lower-income community. She also needed to try to take on a leadership role in Model UN.

- **Academics:** Hayley had a strong academic record, particularly in math and the sciences. She continued to push herself by taking AP classes in those subjects.
- **Test scores:** Hayley initially thought she would favor the ACT with writing, but after disappointing results, she switched to the SATs and hit the ball out of the park, getting into the mid-high 700s in math and critical reading and an 800 on the writing section.
- **Athletics:** Hayley decided to focus on track and cross-country rather than switching to volleyball. She learned a lot about discipline and perseverance from her coach.
- **Special talent:** This was not a piece of Hayley's chart.
- **Intellectual curiosity:** Hayley showed intellectual curiosity in math and science. She pursued that further by attending a six-week pre-college program at Vanderbilt University to home in on some possible career options. She also showed this by participating in Model UN on the Environment and Technology Committee.
- **Leadership:** Hayley worked on developing this through her participation in TASC and becoming a subcommittee chair at Model UN.
- **Other:** Hayley had the potential to be a girl interested in one of the STEM (science, technology, engineering, and math) fields, but she was undecided about her major.
- **Financial:** Hayley did not absolutely need to get merit aid, but it would certainly help.

Developing the College List

Hayley wanted a medium to large university with strong STEM or business majors, an active Greek life, and a strong school spirit. She wanted to major in something in the sciences or business, but her mom was pushing her toward engineering because of future job prospects, so we identified schools that offered strong programs in both engineering and business.

Key College Criteria for Hayley

- Medium to large university
- Location not a critical factor, but wanted to be near a big city or a town
- Wanted to study science, business, or engineering
- Name of the school was important
- Financial aid was not a deal breaker, but it would be nice to get some merit aid
- Wanted to join a sorority and have strong school spirit and sports

The Final List

The Reaches

- **University of Virginia:** UVA has a great reputation and the size is good as well. Hayley liked the feel of the school and the fact that it has strong business and engineering programs.
- **Northwestern University:** This is another great medium-sized school. Hayley was basing this on the reputation of the school and the strong pre-professional programs.

The Possibles

- **University of Michigan:** Hayley liked the big "rah-rah" aspect of Michigan, along with the excellent academics. Since she was applying to the School of Engineering, it became a possible and not a likely choice, given that engineering is a more competitive major.
- **Vanderbilt University:** Hayley spent six weeks at Vandy over the summer at PAVE, a pre-college program, and liked the feel of the campus. However, she was not 100 percent sure it was the school for her.

- **Washington University in St. Louis:** Hayley liked the atmosphere at WashU, but not sure if it was going to be "rah-rah" enough for her.

The Likelies

- **University of Texas at Austin:** Hayley was very comfortable with UT because her older sister was there. She also had family in Texas. She loved Austin and also liked that UT has strong business and engineering programs, particularly environmental engineering, which was the direction she was leaning.
- **Lehigh University:** Hayley felt comfortable with the student body and it was close to home.
- **University of Maryland at College Park:** Hayley knew a lot of people from her school who went to UMD and felt comfortable with the atmosphere. She liked the "rah-rah" aspect and strong business and engineering options.
- **University of Wisconsin:** Hayley liked the feel of Wisconsin and Madison. It also has strong engineering and business programs.

The Safety

- **Tulane University:** Hayley anticipated getting a substantial merit scholarship based on grades and outstanding test scores. She also liked the feel of the school.

Choosing an Essay Topic

After brainstorming with Hayley about her strengths and interests, we identified several areas that she wanted to communicate within her application:

- With freedom comes responsibility: She learned this while on a trip to Israel where she had a lot of freedom, but also realized that she had to act responsibly since there were others in the group.

- She liked to push herself and set internal goals, but she did not like to compete with others.
- Her ability to learn from her mistakes: When she first started cross-country, she was cutting corners and the coach told her she had to push harder to improve. She learned this lesson again in honors pre-calculus when she got a D on the first test and pushed herself to change her study habits and go in for extra help. She ended the year with a B+ in the course.
- Her interest in working with and learning from others: JCC, Jewish summer camp, and a trip to Israel.
- Hayley was still uncertain about her major when we started the process, but her mom was pushing her to apply for engineering.

Narrowing Down Possible Topics

Experience: Hayley's Major Experiences and Their Impacts

- **Track and cross-country teams** (taught her to push herself to continually improve and gave her a sense of community). Hayley joined the track and cross-country teams during her freshman year mostly to have something to do. However, she soon found that she enjoyed the camaraderie of the team and started listening to her coach's pep talks. She became more diligent not only in running but also in her schoolwork.
- **Trip to Israel** (opened her eyes to different levels of Jewish observance). Hayley had never been out of the United States before and she was surprised by how different the cultures were. She got to interact with Israeli teens, and since there was a language barrier, she had to push outside of her comfort zone to find a way to connect. She was also surprised by how intensely people were praying at the Western Wall in Jerusalem. It made her realize how strongly some people feel about their religion and how impervious they are to the perceptions of others.

- **Pre-college program at Vanderbilt University** (exposed her to different career paths and provided her with insight about her strengths). She had the opportunity to explore engineering, medicine, and business. She particularly enjoyed learning about advertising and marketing. She also completed the Myers-Briggs personality-type test, which suggested she was kind, task-oriented, and not domineering.

Issue: Personal, Local, National, or International Issue and Its Importance to Hayley

- **Model UN** (developed leadership and interest in the environment). Hayley became interested in the environment through her participation in Model UN as a member and co-chair of the Environment and Technology Committee. It made her aware of how much we need to work on sustainable energy to protect the planet.

Person: Individuals Who Have Had a Significant Impact on Hayley's Life and Outlook

- **History teacher and coach** (taught her not to cut corners). Her freshman history teacher was also her track and cross-country coach. He was always telling students that if they cut corners, they only hurt themselves. She did not pay much attention to this in history, but when she joined the cross-country team and saw that she would only improve if she ran the entire track without taking shortcuts and gave it 100 percent, she started to bring this mantra into everything she did. It helped her become successful.
- **Maternal grandmother** (taught her to have a positive outlook). She had a very close relationship with her grandmother, who taught her to always look on the bright side of things. This helped Hayley develop a positive outlook.

```
■ ■ ■ Possible Essay Topic Summary Chart ■ ■ ■
```

Experience and Its Impact
Track and cross-country teams
Found a community with other girls on the team
Trip to Israel
Opened eyes to not only a new culture but helped her see religion in a new light
Vanderbilt pre-college program
Helped clarify academic and career goals
Issue and Its Importance
Sustainability and the environment
Provided another area of intellectual curiosity and possible career path
Person and His or Her Impact
History teacher and coach
Learned not to cut corners and always try her best
Grandmother
Developed a positive outlook on life and always looked for the good in every situation

The Personal Statement Essay

Hayley decided to write about her history teacher and coach's words, which resonated with her at different times in her life and propelled her to do the right thing.

"Only you know the truth of what others cannot see." Initially, I thought nothing of these words my old, seemingly boring freshman history teacher spewed throughout class. Figuring they had no relevance to my life, I easily ignored what I believed to be trite clichés. However, Mr. Smith kept offering these kinds of philosophical quotes every day, and at some point, instead of tuning out, I started to listen.

She related this quote to her experience first in cross-country. She described how she did not really understand the true meaning of this quote until she was running cross-country. Hayley talked about how only she would know if she was running the full length of the track; however, she also knew that her times would not improve if she didn't. So she started running the whole course without cutting corners and ultimately improved her times.

This essay answers the Common Application prompt "Reflect on a time when you challenged a belief or idea. What prompted you to act? Would you make the same decision again?" In this case, Hayley shows how she initially challenged her own belief and then showed how she did in fact make the same decision to challenge her belief when she was in Israel. It also worked for the University of Texas essay prompt "Tell us about someone who has made an impact on your life and explain how and why this person is important to you."

During the summer between her sophomore and junior years, Hayley went to Israel. She tied this together with another quote from Mr. Smith.

> Once I saw the power behind these words, I was inspired to apply this concept to other parts of my life as well. When I attended a five-week trip to Israel with my camp, it was the first time I had total freedom to come and go as I pleased. However, after showing up late and holding up my group, I saw an application for another Smith quote: "With freedom comes responsibility." I realized I needed to approach my freedom with respect to the others on my trip and that it was my responsibility to show up on time.

Hayley showed that she was open to improving and taking advice throughout her life. She also showed how she matured from a freshman to a senior.

The Short Answer

After using the personal statement essay to give an in-depth description of how Hayley matured and grew throughout high school, she wanted to use the short answer to introduce a different aspect of her personality. Within the short answer, Hayley describes her experience with Model UN and talks about how she got involved with the Environmental and Technology Committee. This sets the scene for her "Why this academic interest?" essay later, where she wrote:

> Researching environmental issues and debating possible solutions gave me insight into real-world problems and made me realize that I could learn how to use technology to help prevent environmental problems in the future.

Supplemental Essays by School

Even though she initially had a strong interest in business, Hayley decided (after much urging from her mom) to apply primarily to engineering schools. This was not an easy choice, because when Hayley researched the curriculum for engineering disciplines—for example, mechanical engineering, civil engineering—none of them interested her. However, when she found environmental engineering, she became intrigued by the courses. She realized that her experience as the co-chair of the Environmental and Technology Committee for Model UN had given her a good foundation for this field. She also agreed that it might be a good idea to start with a degree in environmental engineering and then get an MBA later. As a result, many of her schools had a "Why engineering?" essay. This essay became the key for helping her stand out because she was able to tie together her strength in math and science to her experience on the Model UN Environment and Technology Committee.

Why Engineering?/Issue of Importance

This essay required a lot of research on Hayley's part to determine which type of engineering she was interested in. Environmental engineering seemed the most interesting to her largely because she had some experience thinking about it through Model UN and she was taking environmental science as a senior and enjoyed the class.

When I became a member of the Model United Nations club as a high school sophomore, I was randomly assigned to the Environment and Technology Committee. Prior to this placement, I did not hold much awareness about environmental issues. As I started researching and arguing Latvia's position on the issues of environment and technology, I began to realize the huge impact human beings make on the environment through their smallest actions and behaviors. After some serious debates on the topics at issue, I realized just how important the environment is to the survival of all living organisms.

She tied her Model UN involvement with her interest in developing sustainable products to protect the planet to describe an issue of importance for the University of Texas.

These and larger issues such as water contamination and air pollution affect countries and communities all over the world. For example, in Latvia, health issues stem from improper handling and disposal of waste materials, especially when too much waste is sent to landfills. The landfills are incapable of handling such a large amount of waste, and these waste materials begin to pollute the air and cause hazardous health problems. Nations need the tools and resources to help achieve developmental goals, improve their residents' quality of life, and make their communities more economically and environmentally sustainable.

With each of my discoveries I became increasingly impassioned and realized that I could combine my love of science and math with environmental advocacy. I hope to study civil and environmental engineering at UT/Austin and ultimately work on issues related to public health and the environment, as well as the larger issues of acid rain, global warming, and ozone depletion.

For the schools that asked how she would explore her academic interests at their school, she then found specific courses at each of the schools. For the University of Michigan she wrote:

> One of the programs that really caught my interest and seems unique to Michigan is the interdisciplinary Global Change curriculum. I am intrigued by the topics listed in this curriculum, such as climate change and human impact to the environment. In particular, I would want to use my math and analytical skills in classes such as "Environmental Informatics: GIS and Modeling Program." The Environmental Informatics curriculum emphasizes the science and societal issues behind environmental problems, which would allow me to dig deeper into this field of study.

This essay allowed Hayley to show her intellectual curiosity in the application. She submitted a variation of this essay topic to University of Virginia (UVA), University of Michigan, Lehigh, Wisconsin, University of Texas, and Vanderbilt.

Book That Impacted You

Hayley had to write about a book that influenced her and why for the University of Maryland and UVA. She chose to write about *The Last Song* by Nicholas Sparks, which is about a girl whose father has cancer. She chose this book because she read it when she was helping a friend cope with cancer, so she was able to relate to the feelings of wanting to help someone even if they resisted the help. This showed Hayley's caring side.

Complementary Angles

Letters of Recommendation

- Hayley asked her chemistry and Spanish teachers for letters of recommendation because they would show different sides of her academic strengths.

- She also got a letter of recommendation from the track coach who was so instrumental in her development.

Brag Sheet/Resume
- Hayley had a fairly balanced wheel, so her activities demonstrated strength in track, cross-country, community service, and Model UN.
- It also highlighted her STEM involvement through her pre-college PAVE program at Vanderbilt and her involvement with the Environment and Technology Committee of Model UN.

Supplemental Materials
- Hayley had no supplemental materials.

Additional Information
- Hayley did not have any extenuating circumstances to report in her record. She uploaded her detailed brag sheet/resume here.

Results

The Reaches
- **University of Virginia:** Denied
- **Northwestern University:** Denied

The Possibles
- **University of Michigan:** Accepted
- **Vanderbilt University:** Denied
- **Washington University in St. Louis:** Accepted

The Likelies
- **University of Texas at Austin:** Accepted
- **Lehigh University:** Accepted

- **University of Maryland at College Park:** Accepted into honors program
- **University of Wisconsin:** Accepted

The Safety
- **Tulane University:** Accepted with $27,000 per year scholarship

Final Decision
University of Texas at Austin Engineering School

What Can You Learn from Hayley's Story?
Questions to Ask Yourself
- Who is someone who has influenced you or made you think about how you approach life? How have you changed because of this person?
- How has a travel experience changed the way you view yourself or others? How have you changed?
- What are your academic strengths? How can you apply those to a potential major or career?
- How do your extracurricular activities tie into your intended major?
- How can you show a theme that runs through various aspects of your life to create a unique angle?

Notes

CASE STUDY **5**

DAN
THE POLITICAL,
OUTGOING MUSICIAN

Lessons Learned during the Application Process

Dan's profile reveals that getting into college is not always a linear process and may involve a few zigs and zags along the way. Dan shows how important it is to keep at it even if you can't always get what you want—at least not at first. He also shows how important it is when applying to schools based on grades and a special talent to form relationships with professors to help pave the way._

Dan's Snapshot
- GPA: 4.4 (weighted, out of 4.8)
- Rigor: 15 AP/honors classes
- SAT: 1430/2210
- ACT with writing: N/A
- Class rank: top 5 percent

About Dan

- Main interests: jazz music, politics
- Dan was a talented musician and leader. He participated in every musical opportunity available to him in his high school, including marching band, jazz band, and the pit orchestra for his high school's musicals.
- Dan also was a member of a four-person jazz quartet that played at various functions within in the community, both volunteer and for pay.
- He attended a select jazz summer program, Eastern U.S. Music Camp at Colgate University, and was selected as a camp counselor there for the next summer.
- He went to a suburban high school and was well liked among his peers due to his outgoing personality.
- Dan was also very involved in his school's chapter of Junior Statesmen of America (JSA); he was part of the cabinet during his sophomore year and hoped to become president during his junior year.
- He wanted to pursue music in college, but his parents wanted him to have other options as well.

Personality Profile

Dan exuded confidence and friendliness. He had many passions, with music and politics foremost among them. Dan managed multiple activities at school (marching band, jazz band, JSA) and an intense academic schedule, yet he never appeared frazzled. He blended his "cool cat," hipster vibe with academic intensity quite well.

Dan was a balanced student and excelled in all his academic subjects, though math, music, science, and history were his clear favorites. He was very interested in politics, enjoyed participating in JSA, and wanted to become president of the club by his senior year. He also loved anything musical and was a section leader for the saxophones in his school's marching band, hoping to use his natural leadership skills to become a drum major by his senior year.

Most of his community service had been related to his music activities, as his school's elite jazz band often played at community functions. Dan would see if his quartet can play at other community events to boost that side of his profile. Meanwhile, Dan and his mother both had very strong personalities and sometimes clashed when considering the best college route for Dan to follow.

Creating Dan's College Application Wheel

I met Dan during the spring of his sophomore year. He was personable and confident, and had a clear sense of his strengths, in both leadership and music. We discussed Dan's special talent and interest in music, and how he could also bolster his natural leadership skills through his musical pursuits. He had already emerged as a section leader for the saxophones in his school's marching band during his sophomore year, so we set a goal for him to become drum major of the marching band by senior year.

Dan was interested in majoring in music in college, so we discussed the types of colleges where he could pursue his passion, and the kinds of music degrees available—from a bachelor of music degree within a straight music conservatory, to a bachelor of music degree at a university, to a bachelor of arts in music degree at a liberal arts college. Given his varied interests, I suggested that he research all these options and decide which one made the most sense. His parents were pushing for a larger university environment that would provide more options, in case he changed his mind and no longer wanted to pursue music exclusively.

Since Dan also had an interest in history and politics, we set a goal for him to become president of JSA by his senior year, so he would have depth in that area to balance out his music special talent area. It would also underscore his leadership skills by going deep in his two passions: music and politics. Further involvement in JSA would also show his intellectual curiosity, since it is an academic club.

Academically, Dan was an excellent student. He had challenged himself consistently by taking only honors classes throughout his sophomore year. But he did not enjoy French and found it to be his most challenging class, so he decided to take regular French during junior year and remain in honors for every other subject. It made sense for him to focus his energy on classes of interest. I suggested that he determine whether he preferred the ACT with writing test or the SAT. His goal was to get a 31+ for the ACT or score in the 700s for each section of the SATs in order to match his academic transcript. His PSAT scores were well below those challenging goals, so Dan would need to study hard and get some additional tutoring assistance to reach them. I suggested that he take the chemistry and US history subject tests in June of his sophomore year, since he was enrolled in honors chemistry and AP history that year.

Given Dan's extremely busy schedule, he did not have a lot of time for community service outside of what he was doing with his school's elite jazz band. We talked about finding other ways to perform music within the community, but we did not feel like this area would be a stumbling block as he was already so active in his school community.

Dan's Strengths

- Special talent in music
- Leadership prowess in multiple venues
- Strong, well-rounded student
- Hardworking and motivated
- High grades in challenging curriculum
- Strong sense of confidence and purpose
- Intellectual curiosity in politics and music

Dan's Weaknesses

- Limited time for community service
- Test scores
- Music could be double-edged sword, because he would need to match academics and music for highly select schools

Dan's Checklist

Dan had a strong academic record. His goal was to continue with a rigorous curriculum while advancing his musical and leadership skills. He would also have to carve out time to prepare for the SAT to reach his goal of 700+ on each section of the test.

Dan would have to take regular French and English in his senior year to give him time to focus his energy on the courses that he enjoyed more, such as math, science, and history, as well as to bolster his intellectual curiosity through his involvement in JSA and music. I suggested that he should also pursue his natural leadership skills by becoming president of JSA, drum major for marching band, and a camp counselor at his summer music camp. This would show that Dan had contributed in a meaningful way during high school and would most likely continue to do so once he got into college.

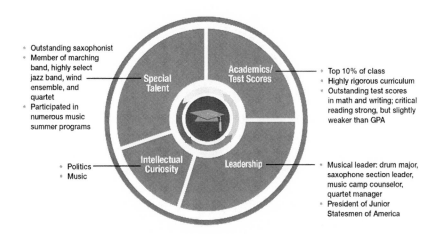

Dan's Application Wheel: Fall of Senior Year

- **Academics:** Dan had a strong academic record, getting straight A's in every subject. He needed to continue to push himself by taking Advanced Placement or honors classes in his areas of interest and strength—honors physics, AP government, AP economics, and AP calculus BC—but give himself some breathing room by taking regular English and no French senior year, since he completed his fourth year of French during his junior year.

- **Test scores:** Dan reached his goal in the math and writing section of the SATs, but his critical reading score fell into the mid-600s. Dan took the test one more time and increased his critical reading by fifty points. He still fell ten points below his 700 goal, but he did not want to take the test again. This was a risk, but he hoped that his special talent and stellar transcript would outweigh this score, since his math score was 740 and his writing score was 790. He also scored in the 700s in the chemistry and US history SAT subject tests.

- **Athletics:** This was not part of Dan's chart.

- **Special talent:** Dan clearly stood out in this area. He had tremendous depth as a member, section leader, and drum major of his school's marching band; as a jazz band member; as a saxophonist in the pit orchestra; and as a leader of his own jazz quartet. Dan had also attended summer music camp for three years and was selected to be a camp counselor at the same camp. He also enjoyed composing and listening to music on his own.

- **Intellectual curiosity:** Dan had a keen interest in politics and closely followed the 2012 election. He developed this further through his involvement as president of JSA and by taking AP government. He also read political news websites and was interested in the unfolding fiscal crisis.

- **Leadership:** Dan had strong depth of leadership in multiple arenas; he was drum major for the marching band, section leader for the jazz band, music camp counselor, president of JSA, and manager of his jazz quartet.

- **Other:** He had some legacy at Columbia University and Cornell University, since his parents went to graduate school at those schools.

- **Financial:** Dan did not have a financial need; however, his parents assigned value to certain schools where they are willing to pay the full cost. They would, of course, welcome merit aid where available and make the final decision based on perceived value.

Developing the College List

Music—and more specifically, the quality of a school's jazz studies program—became a primary driver for the development of Dan's college list. He and his mom initially were in conflict about how important the music program should be in determining the list. For example, Dan's mom wanted music to be available, but did not necessarily think that it should be the sole criterion for selecting a college. Dan, on the other hand, wanted a strong academic school, but for him, the quality and availability of the jazz studies curriculum and faculty was of utmost importance. This ruled out straight conservatories, and so we focused on schools with outstanding music offerings, which also provided strong opportunities for classes in a wide range of subjects—politics, science, and the liberal arts.

We also had to weigh the differences between a bachelor of music degree and a bachelor of arts in music degree, and how much the audition counted toward acceptance. A bachelor of music degree is comparable to a conservatory education, whereas a bachelor of arts in music degree typically does not require an audition. In the latter case, students select music as their major, much as they would select English or chemistry. Dan and his mom spent a lot of time researching the jazz studies program at various schools, and whenever possible met with a professor from the jazz department during each of their visits. I also recommended that Dan take a lesson from a music professor or, if possible, listen to the groups perform that he intended to join, so he could start building a relationship with the faculty.

Key College Criteria for Dan

- A medium-sized school, one between 5,000 and 15,000 students, that offered a wide range of academic, social, and musical opportunities
- Easy access to his professors, so he could build close relationships with them
- Opportunity to study jazz music, and possibly science, politics, or pre-law
- Name of the school was important
- Thought it would be fun to have a big "rah-rah" sports culture and some Greek life available, but this did not drive his initial college list
- Definitely wanted a strong jazz band, jazz combo, or wind ensemble
- A down-to-earth, diverse, liberal student body, as well as like-minded musically oriented students
- Financial aid would not impact his initial list of schools, but merit aid was welcome.
- Quality of the jazz music program and the energy of the school were critical factors

Because Dan applied directly to the music school at the majority of the schools on his list, he added an extra layer for admissions: He needed to be admitted not only academically, but also musically. To complicate his list more, these two areas did not always align in their degree of difficulty. For example, some schools were reaches for Dan musically, but quite likely academically, and vice versa. Finally, given that Dan loved the University of North Carolina at Chapel Hill, he did not want to apply early decision to any other school, even though he knew it would increase his chances. But he did end up applying early action, because of the musical audition component, and he was deferred at schools that required an audition. As a result, he ended up with a list that was top heavy in possible and reach schools, and prepared himself to accept the consequences of a challenging admissions process.

Dan's Final List

The Reaches: Music/Academic

- **Cornell University:** Cornell is considered to have the best music program of the Ivies (according to a jazz professor), and Dan had legacy through his dad.

- **University of North Carolina at Chapel Hill:** Dan fell in love with the vibe of UNC, the music program, and the academics. He liked the fact that its size was big enough to have outstanding opportunities and energy, but not so big that he would get lost. His mom was concerned that it was difficult to get in as an out-of-state student, and that he might feel out of place as there were so many students from North Carolina.

The Reaches: Music

- **University of Maryland at College Park:** UMD was a likely academically, but a reach in music. Dan's academic record and activities placed him at the high end of the UMD applicant pool, and he would likely get into its honors program. It has an outstanding jazz program, and Dan wanted to see if he could get into it. But he would only go to UMD if he got into their music program; otherwise, he did not feel it was the best fit.

- **University of Miami:** Dan also loved Miami's music department, but did not feel as comfortable overall as he did at UNC Chapel Hill.

The Reach.: Academic

- **Duke University:** This was not on Dan's original list, but he decided to throw it in at the end just for the heck of it.

The Possibles

- **University of Virginia:** Dan had a good connection with the jazz professor there and felt that he fit in well musically and that his music might give him an edge even though he was from out of state.

- **Emory University:** Dan liked Emory and thought he could get his needs met there. His mom loved the feel of Emory.

- **Tufts University:** This was a school that Dan threw in to please his mom.

- **University of California at Los Angeles:** Dan loved the thought of going to school in California and liked what he read about UCLA. He secretly applied to their School of Arts and Sciences with his dad's blessing. (His mom did not want him going so far from home, so he did not tell her that he applied until after the fact.)

- **University of California at Berkeley:** Since UCLA and UC Berkeley share the same application, he also applied here as a "why not?" school.

- **Vanderbilt University:** He liked Vanderbilt, but their music program is more classical than jazz. His mom thought he should apply early decision to increase his chances (which was true); however, he would not hear back from UNC until January, and therefore was not willing to let go of his dream school.

The Likely

- **University of Delaware:** Dan liked its music program and thought he would be happy in its honors college, too.

The Safety

- **Tulane University:** Dan applied to Tulane because he knew it had stellar academics and a solid jazz program. The city of New Orleans also appealed to him. He would likely get merit aid there, as well.

Choosing an Essay Topic

After brainstorming with Dan about his strengths and interests, we identified several areas that he wanted to communicate in his application.

- Even though he had focused most of his energy on music, he also had a lot of interests outside of music that influenced him, such as politics and science.

- Dan always kept moving, even with setbacks. His dogged persistence guided him; at times, he said he could seem pushy, but he learned that with everything bad comes something good, so he kept moving forward.

- He was down-to-earth, but organized and firm in his resolve. He showed this through serving as drum major for the marching band, managing his musical quartet, and carving his own path outside of his parents' definition of success.

- Music taught him to see life without boundaries, because he learned to adapt a musical piece beyond the printed music. When Dan played, especially when he played jazz, he often discovered new ways to interpret the music. He applied that thinking to everything he did in life, from leading the Junior Statesmen of America club, to class discussions, to interacting with his peers.

- Music also taught him how to get along with a wide range of people and introduced him to many different worlds.

Narrowing Down Possible Essay Topics

Experience: Dan's Major Experiences and Their Impacts

- **Almost quitting music in the sixth grade, because he did not like the teacher** (this helped him realize that he shouldn't let a bad teacher prevent him from doing what he loves). In the sixth grade, Dan wanted to quit playing music because he did not like his band teacher and many of his friends started dropping out. But his seventh and eighth grade teacher encouraged him to stick it out and asked him to switch to tenor saxophone and join the jazz band. Once he made the switch, there was no turning back. He had found his passion in music. It made him realize that he has to give things a second chance. He decided from then on to pursue what he loves and not let a negative person get in his way.

- **Getting kicked out of his five-person band going into freshman year** (this put him on a new path—joining the marching band—which became a major influence in his life). Dan had a group of best friends from middle school with whom he played in a band, and while he was away at summer camp, they decided they preferred playing without him. This betrayal upset him at first, but then he joined the marching band. He did not know anyone, but he had an open mind and soon he found himself part of a community like none he had ever known. He learned that when times are tough, he has to remain positive and open to new experiences.

- **Making music** (Dan realized that people make music together). Half the battle in creating music is good interaction between the musicians, and Dan learned how to be an exceptional leader by being around musicians and meeting their high expectations. Participating in so many musical groups taught Dan how to interact with people who share a common ground, and he has used that knowledge to interact with others outside of music. He also learned that it's not technology that furthers being a good musician, but being a good person.

- **Junior Statesmen of America** (Dan realized that he can still have a good time when leading). The previous president of JSA had a dogmatic, top-down leadership style, which alienated many of the club's members. When Dan became president of the club, he wanted to lead differently, in a more collaborative way, based on his experience in various musical groups. Dan also realized that he could still have fun when leading, and that if others liked him, he could manage more effectively, as long as he garnered their respect by being firm and fair. He also enlisted his fellow club members' ideas to make them feel part of the club.

- **Arranging the musical piece "Sleep" by Eric Whitacre.** Dan heard this piece for the first time at music camp and it blew him away. The piece was beautiful, with highly complex, crazy, dissonant harmonies that amazed him. It was surprising how musical these sounds could be. It showed him how to be calm in the face of craziness.

Issue: Personal, Local, National, or International Issue and Its Importance to Dan

- **Congress and the fiscal crisis.** Dan watched the fiscal crisis unfold while on vacation and was dismayed by the way politicians put their own interests ahead of the greater good. He had always been interested in politics, but after watching Congress fail to reach an agreement, he became disgusted by the whole process and wanted to find a way to effect change in the system.

Person: Individuals Who Have Had a Significant Impact on Dan's Life and Outlook

- **Middle school band teacher** (rekindled his love of music). His band teacher showed Dan how to continue doing something that he loved, despite an unpleasant teacher. He also helped him discover music as a form of expression and how to give it feeling. As a result, Dan became fascinated by musical sounds and learned that there is never a boundary in music. He applied that lesson to his own life.
- **Parents** (emphasized hard work and the power of a plan B). Dan's parents worked very hard and always emphasized the importance of hard work, education, and being well rounded. Dan agreed, to some extent, but he also wanted to find passion and happiness in his work. He felt like his parents worked really hard but did not really relax. His goal was to find work that he loves, so that he can work hard but also be happy.
- **Robert** (a junior who welcomed Dan as a freshman into his school's marching band). Robert mentored Dan musically and exposed him to various jazz musicians, such as Kenny Garrett and Chris Potter.

■ ■ ■ **Possible Essay Topic Summary Chart** ■ ■ ■

Experience and Its Impact

Being kicked out of band prior to high school

Forced him to join marching band, which turned out to be a pivotal experience in his life

Variety of musical experiences

Taught him how to collaborate with others and broaden his perspective, both inside and outside of music

JSA president

Gave him another leadership outlet; he found a way to apply his leadership skills in a different arena

Issue and Its Importance

Politics

Saw how lack of collaboration leads to discord

Person and His or Her Impact

Middle school band teacher

Showed him how to recover from a setback and, more important, opened him up to his passion for music

Parents

Modeled success but also made him confident enough to forge his own path to success

Robert

Exposed him to a new world within marching band and jazz

The Personal Statement Essay

Dan expressed himself naturally through music, not words, so writing his personal statement posed a challenge. He knew that he wanted to show how his love for music and collaboration influenced his leadership style and his ability to interact with people, though he had a hard time describing this in words at first. But after several drafts, he found his voice. Dan described how his jazz quartet transformed a hard rock song into a jazz ballad, and the magical feeling he got from working collaboratively to create something unique and even better.

I had a vision of the song being like a story map, complete with rising action, a climax, and falling action. I kept the original melody intact, but added a jazz texture and intricate harmonies with my saxophone. Meanwhile, my piano and bass player added a chromatic phrase (notes that are very close in tonality to each other) to the bridge of the song. Then we had to turn up the drama and fun of the song to bring back more of the original spirit. Collaboratively, we decided the most powerful way to do this would be by altering the volume levels throughout the piece.

By the end, I felt we had transformed as much as our song. It was extraordinary to see what could be produced working together as a group. I felt energized to have creatively taken something ordinary and altered it into something fresh.

In his essay, Dan showcased not only his knowledge and passion for music, but also his excitement for collaborative creation. This became a theme in his application: his ability to transmit his passion to others and work with them to build something better. The second half of his essay showed how he applied what he learned from his musical quartet to serving as president of the JSA.

As president of JSA, I took a more collaborative approach; rather than limiting the generation of ideas and debates to a few handpicked members, I provided an open forum for all members to express their ideas. I left a hat out for people to submit their ideas on a slip of paper whenever they came up with one. I found that creating a friendly, participatory environment and attitude not only made the members enjoy the club more, but it also encouraged them to be more flexible about debate topics and be more involved in the club.

His essay worked with the Common Application prompt "Describe a place or environment where you are perfectly content. What do you do or experience there, and why is it meaningful to you?" In this instance,

Dan described an environment of creative collaboration and showed two different environments where his leadership allowed his special talent and intellectual curiosity to thrive. He concluded his essay:

> Music has shown me how I can take something that seems humdrum and turn it into something compelling and creative. It's shaped my leadership style, and me as a person. It demonstrates that boundaries only exist in my mind, and with an innovative spin and a little help from my friends, I can make something ordinary into something extraordinary.

Dan effectively showed, with concrete, varied examples, how his leadership philosophy of removing boundaries would help him make any college community extraordinary.

The Short Answer

Dan was asked to write about one of his activities in more detail. He chose to provide another example of musical leadership in this essay by describing how he conducted his school's marching band as drum major. Marching band played a significant role in Dan's high school experience, and this essay gave him the opportunity to explain how and why he loved marching band.

> "Drum major, is the band ready?" I salute the audience and turn to face the 150-person band on the field. Rather than being nervous, I am excited and focused. As the drum major, no matter what happens, it is my job to keep the group together and guide them through the show. I determine the tempo in my head and count off the band. As the show begins, I scan the field to find some 300 eyes on me. I keep my beats steady and clear, allowing the members on the field to bring the music to life. I take mental notes of parts that were well executed and parts that need work, so I can report to my band director later. There is always room to improve; it is my role to push the band as far as they can go.

In the paragraph above, Dan provided another example of how he pushed boundaries and developed his leadership style.

Supplemental Essays by School

Dan had several supplemental essays to write for his list of schools that were on the Common Application as well as state schools that did not participate in the Common Application, such as UCLA and UC Berkeley.

These essays fell into six categories:

- Why this school? (Tufts, University of Miami)
- Why music/this academic interest? (University of Miami, Tufts)
- Why this school and major? (Emory, Cornell, Duke)
- What is your latest discovery, and what do you hope to learn next? (UNC, UMD)
- Describe the world you come from, and how that shaped you. (UCLA, UC Berkeley, UVA, Tufts)
- Describe a piece of art, music, or literature that surprised you. (UVA)

Why This School and Major? (and Variations on This Theme)

This essay required Dan to be very specific about the qualities of each school that fit his personality. For the schools he was applying to for music, he focused on the interactions with professors that he had during his visits and through continued correspondence. He also identified which musical groups he would join and highlighted his non-music-related academic interests, and how those could be fulfilled at said school. Once he wrote this essay, he could easily tailor it for each school and its offerings.

What Is Your Latest Discovery and What Do You Hope to Learn Next?

This became a great question for Dan to showcase his non-musical interests and highlight his intellectual curiosity. He described how he was on vacation watching the news coverage of the debt-ceiling crisis and was saddened to see how divisive our country had become from a political perspective.

> While on vacation in Mexico this past summer, I witnessed the debt-ceiling crisis unfold from my hotel room television. I watched with frustration as reporters talked of the arguments occurring inside our Congress. It seemed to me that President Obama was giving in to all the Republicans requests, while the Republicans themselves refused to budge. I kept waiting for the members of our government to put the welfare of the country in front of partisan interests, but the result was disappointing. I discovered American politics has become more divided than united.

He then went on to describe how this stimulated his interest in learning even more about our political system and what he would do at each school to continue this pursuit.

> I want to discover not only how our political system works, but also how to bring the parties together. At UNC I can learn how the president works with Congress to make decisions affecting our country by taking classes like "Political Economy I: The Domestic System," or "The President, Congress, and Public Policy." I can get involved with the American Politics Research Group to dig deeper and get behind the scenes of our government. I can listen to "in-progress" work done by prominent political researchers to learn some very well-supported opinions about the direction our country is headed. Finally, I can interact with diverse students with varying points of view with the hope that one day I can help get our political system back on track.

Dan's specificity and passion came through in this essay and showed the admissions committees how he would contribute to the community academically and socially. He also had the foundation for part of his academic interest essay.

Family Background and Influence

Dan used this essay to describe his relationship with his parents and how they always pushed him to work hard academically and had encouraged his musical interests—as a hobby. However, when he wanted to pursue music in a more serious way, their definitions of success had diverged. Dan talked about how he nevertheless stood strong in his efforts to follow his passion, and how he would adhere to his parents' values about hard work but defined success on his own terms.

Music That Surprised You

He talked about a piece of choral music that moved him in a surprising way.

> I first heard Eric Whitacre's "Sleep" at Eastern U.S. Music Camp. As soon as the choir began, I was absolutely awestruck that the human voice alone could produce such a glorious sound.

Dan then went on to describe how this piece opened up a new world of music to him, inspiring him to adapt it for his brass quartet—again showing that he would always push beyond set boundaries to create something new.

Complementary Angles

Letters of Recommendation
- Dan asked his chemistry teacher to write a letter of recommendation because he could speak about Dan's work ethic; he also asked his English teacher because she could address his creativity.
- Dan got a supplemental letter from a music advisor who spoke to his leadership and musical talent.

Brag Sheet/Resume
- For his resume, Dan went extremely deep in music and leadership. He outlined the many musical experiences he had and showcased his progressive leadership responsibilities in each.
- He also went deep in his involvement with Junior Statesmen of America and was able to show that on his resume.

Supplemental Materials
- This was a critical component of Dan's application and was designed to highlight his musical prowess. He prepared a CD and web link to demonstrate his musical abilities.
- For those schools that required an audition, he prepared pieces according to the requirements specified on each school's website and then auditioned.
- He also kept up an ongoing email conversation with professors in the music departments of the schools he was interested in regarding his interest. He developed a particularly strong relationship with professors from UNC and UVA.

Additional Information
- Dan did not have any extenuating circumstances to report in his record. He uploaded his detailed resume here.

Results

The Reaches: Music/Academic
- **Cornell University:** Denied
- **University of North Carolina at Chapel Hill:** Deferred early action; waitlisted regular decision

The Reaches: Music
- **University of Maryland at College Park:** Accepted into honors program but denied music
- **University of Miami:** Accepted but denied music

The Reach: Academic
- **Duke University:** Denied

The Possibles
- **University of Virginia:** Deferred early action; waitlisted regular decision
- **Emory University:** Waitlisted
- **Tufts University:** Denied
- **University of California Los Angeles:** Accepted
- **University of California at Berkeley:** Accepted
- **Vanderbilt University:** Waitlisted

The Likely
- **University of Delaware:** Accepted music and honors programs

The Safety
- **Tulane University:** Accepted ($27,000 merit scholarship)

Final Decision

The final decision became difficult, because even though Dan had some fabulous options, he was still waitlisted at his top choice, UNC Chapel Hill. To compound the confusion, the jazz music professor with whom Dan had developed a relationship was continuing to email him and let him know that he was very interested in him and really wanted to see him at UNC. (*Okay*, Dan thought, *then do what you can to get me in!*)

Dan remained positive and upbeat throughout this process, even in the face of disappointment. We talked about his other options and he narrowed it down to UCLA ("awesome school!") and Tulane ("awesome scholarship!"). He went back to visit each of them, and when he stepped onto the UCLA campus he felt the same excitement and energy that he did at UNC. It didn't hurt that the weather was amazing and that the girl who showed him around was especially attractive. He did not get the same vibe at Tulane; however, his parents found it hard to pass up the very significant merit money.

Dan was thrilled to go to UCLA, but his parents insisted that it was too far away and too expensive compared to Tulane and pointed out that he was not in the music school since he applied to the College of Letters and Science. As a result, Dan felt betrayed by the process. But this is where his dogged persistence paid off. He put together a PowerPoint presentation convincing his parents to let him go to UCLA. They agreed because they saw how much he wanted to go to that school, and they admitted that it was a great fit with an outstanding reputation. Dan sent in his deposit for UCLA, happy that he had such a great option, considering that he had applied surreptitiously to the school.

Meanwhile, he continued to correspond with the jazz professor at UNC because we still felt like he had a chance to get off the wait list. The jazz professor again told Dan that he really liked him and would love to see him at UNC. So Dan called him and told him that UNC was still his top choice and asked him what, if anything, he could do to help him get off the wait list. The professor asked him where he ultimately enrolled and Dan told him UCLA. The professor then said, "What the heck! We can't lose you to UCLA. Let me speak with admissions." The next day, Dan got a call telling him he was in! So he withdrew his acceptance from UCLA and gladly sent in his deposit to matriculate at his dream school, UNC Chapel Hill. Both he and his mom were ecstatic.

Postscript: When Dan got to UNC and spoke with the professor, he learned that a California drummer whom the music department had recommended for admissions as one of their top choices (Dan was the first alternate) had been accepted at both UNC and UCLA. This Californian loved UNC too, but ultimately chose UCLA because all his family members had gone there. So when the professor found out that Dan, whom he had supported all along, was also going to go to UCLA, he couldn't let that happen. Ironically, it was Dan's application to UCLA that helped him realize his dream in an unexpected, roundabout way.

What Can You Learn from Dan's Story?
Questions to Ask Yourself

- What themes run through your life? How can you find those themes expressed in many different life experiences?
- How did you develop your leadership style? How have you demonstrated leadership in multiple arenas?
- What drives you? How is this different from what drives your parents? How can you forge your own path for success?
- How do you react to setbacks? How do you continue to move ahead in the face of adversity? How has this ability influenced your path to success?
- Do you have a special talent? How have your nurtured it? How can you use it to differentiate yourself from others?
- How can you forge relationships with others to help you succeed?

Notes

6

KADEN
THE TRANSGENDER
ACTIVIST FILMMAKER

Lessons Learned during the Application Process

In this case, you will see how Kaden managed through several difficult personal issues, but ultimately showed his natural leadership and creativity. You will also see how starting at a community college can work to your advantage if you have to stay close to home to take care of family members or if you have a rocky high school record. Ultimately, Kaden's case will demonstrate how natural leadership skills and the willingness to be an agent for change work to your advantage regardless of circumstances.

Kaden's Snapshot

- GPA: 2.8 (weighted, out of 4.3)
- Rigor: 3 AP/honors classes
- SAT: 1150/1700
- ACT with writing: N/A
- Class rank: bottom 50 percent

About Kaden

- Main interests: politics, film, social activism
- During the first half of high school, Kaden identified as female.
- Kaden was very involved and invigorated by politics and worked on Hillary Clinton's presidential campaign in 2008.
- He is a talented musician. He played the violin in several orchestras and teaches violin.
- Kaden struggled with gender identity issues and came out as transgender during junior year. These personal struggles impacted his grades during high school.
- He has intellectual curiosity for film, politics, and serving as a change agent.
- He changed focus and interests midway through the college search process from initial interest in politics to interest in colleges that would support transgender students to finally looking for colleges with a strong film program.
- Kaden's father became sick during senior year of high school.

Personality Profile

Kaden spent the fall of sophomore year campaigning for US presidential candidate Hillary Clinton, and the experience invigorated him. He was clearly intellectually curious and passionate, but had not translated this passion into a strong academic record. His grades were inconsistent, a smattering of mostly B's mixed with A's and C's, and a D in AP politics. He promised to go in for extra help in school to improve his grades so that his transcript would match his passion. He showed signs of leadership through his continued interest in politics, initially with the Clinton campaign and later by securing an internship at a local New Jersey congressman's office. He derived a lot of satisfaction from non-school-related activities.

He was also an accomplished musician, playing the violin in several orchestras. Both of his parents were musicians, so he grew up playing music. He also taught violin to several local students.

Creating Kaden's College Application Wheel

At our first meeting, Kaden was excited about pursuing a career in politics behind the scenes. He spoke passionately about his experience working for the Clinton campaign and as a result signed up for AP government. Unfortunately, Kaden was unable to translate his success in the field to success in the classroom because he found the material and rate of learning overwhelming. We talked about going in for extra help and trying to bring up his grade to at least a C. Several months passed between our meetings.

Kaden's Strengths

- Intellectual curiosity fueled by a passion for politics
- Great experience working as an intern for Hillary Clinton's campaign and local congressman
- Resourceful
- Strong leader
- Musical talent
- In touch with himself and his needs

Kaden's Weaknesses

- Grades and test scores did not reflect intellectual promise
- Had not performed in more challenging classes
- Struggled with a lot of personal issues that made it harder to focus on schoolwork

Kaden's Checklist

Kaden had strong extracurricular activities and experiential learning; however, his academic record was weak. While he is generally good in math, he fell asleep during the New Jersey High School Proficiency Assessment exams and scored below proficient in math. Therefore he had to take remedial math at the same time he took pre-calculus. Kaden was also not performing well in AP government, so he needed to go in for extra help and develop different study skills to bring his grade up. He also needed to start studying for the SATs with a private tutor or class to help boost his academic profile.

Kaden was counseled to continue his political pursuits over the summer to show a depth in this area and to continue playing the violin in the Greater Newark Youth Orchestra and teaching lessons. Kaden's leadership and initiative would illustrate that he would be able to contribute to a college community.

The next time we met, as our discussion progressed and we reviewed the list of colleges, it became clear that the previous strategy no longer applied. Kaden had come up with a new list of seemingly disparate colleges that did not fit our previous discussions. As I probed deeper into the attraction to these particular schools, it came out that these schools interested Kaden because they paid for transgender operations for their students.

During Kaden's senior year, several major events occurred: He realized that he was transgender (a boy inside a girl's body), he got involved in a documentary film about transgender teens and became fascinated by the director and overall process of making a film, and his father was diagnosed with cancer. Because of these life-altering events, Kaden chose to stay at home for his first year of college and attend Union County College, a local community college.

We met again during the fall of his freshman year at UCC with the intention of transferring to a four-year college with a strong film program. The Kaden who greeted me now appeared self-assured and invigorated. He spoke excitedly about his experience working on a transgender teen documentary with a graduate film student at NYU. One of his friends suggested that he audition for a role in the film even though he had never acted before. He found his calling behind the camera through assisting the director of the film. This experience inspired him to create a YouTube video blog about his own experience as a transgender person and changing identity from female to male. The YouTube project took off, garnering thousands of views, and Kaden found his voice as an agent for change.

Based on his positive experience chronicling his gender change, Kaden created a series of local meet-ups for LGBTQ teens run exclusively by teens. He wanted LGBTQ teens to have a safe haven to come and hang out, share their lives, and feel comfortable. This too became extremely popular and Kaden found his calling again as a leader.

Kaden's Strengths (Revised)

- Grades and test scores improved while at community college
- Had a strong portfolio to show for film schools
- Intellectual curiosity fueled by a passion for film
- Great experience working as an intern for film director for transgender documentary on teens
- Took a risk by creating YouTube chronicling his transformation
- Strong leadership exhibited by creating LGBTQ meet-ups
- Musical talent
- In touch with himself and his needs

Kaden's Weaknesses (Revised)

- Grades from high school were likely not strong enough for most competitive film schools

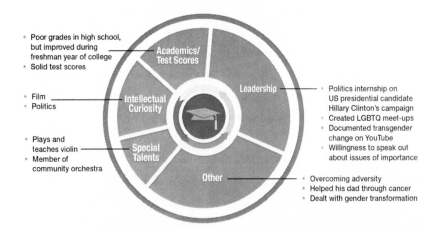

Kaden's Transfer Application Wheel: Fall of Freshman Year of College

- **Academics:** Kaden got mostly B's during his first year at Union County College, which would hopefully be enough proof that he was academically ready and override his high school grades.
- **Test scores:** His test scores were solid, but a little low for most competitive film schools.
- **Athletics:** This was not part of Kaden's pie.
- **Special talent:** This was a large part of his pie as both a filmmaker and musician. He could illustrate his talent by submitting a portfolio of his films.
- **Intellectual curiosity:** Kaden showed intellectual curiosity on numerous levels outside of the classroom, starting with his fascination with politics and bringing that same drive and passion to film and LGBTQ rights.
- **Leadership:** Kaden's creation and leadership of the LGBTQ meet-ups underscored his strong leadership. He also showed leadership through his involvement with assistant directing the documentary on transgender teens.
- **Other:** Kaden showed remarkable strength of character. His ability to take his personal issues and not only deal with them but also use them to help others deal with them was extraordinary. He also stayed home to go to college his first year so that he could help his family while his father was undergoing cancer treatment. This ability to overcome adversity and turn it into something positive emphasized how Kaden would positively contribute to any college community.
- **Financial:** Kaden's family preferred to keep the costs similar to an in-state option, but said that the cost would not impact where he went.

Developing the College List

Kaden wanted a school renowned for its film program with a flexible enough curriculum that he could take classes outside of film as well. He wanted a community that would be open-minded and accepting.

Key College Criteria for Kaden

- Strong BFA or BA in film
- Name of the school was not as important as the fit
- Open, tolerant community
- Cost was not on overriding factor, but he preferred to stay within the cost of a public state option
- Would be nice if they accepted his transfer credits from UCC

The Final List

The Reaches

- **Tisch School of the Arts at New York University:** NYU has one of the top film schools in the country, and Kaden had experience working with the director from its graduate film school. Kaden's grades and test scores were well below what NYU looks for, but talent counts for 50 percent of the admissions score. His brother was an alumnus.
- **American University:** This school has a strong film program and is close to DC in case his political passion resurfaced.
- **Emerson College:** Emerson is another top film school, and Kaden liked the idea of being in Boston.

The Possible

- **SUNY Purchase:** Kaden really liked this school when he visited. He felt very comfortable in the environment, it has a top film school (Purchase offers both a BFA and BA in film option), it is close to Manhattan and home, and the price was affordable.

The Likelies

- **Drexel University:** Drexel has a good film program, and Kaden liked the hands-on curriculum.
- **Rutgers University:** This was a good financial safety for Kaden, and while not a small school, it has a strong film program.

- **Hofstra University:** Hofstra has a strong film program and good location near Manhattan.

The Safety
- **City University of New York at Brooklyn:** This school has a good film program, and the location and price were right.

Choosing an Essay Topic

After brainstorming with Kaden about his strengths and interests, we identified several areas that he wanted to communicate within his application.

- Passion for politics and film and desire to effect change.
- Journey to discovering his true self and his voice, first through politics, then as a transgender person through YouTube videos, and finally as a filmmaker.
- Leadership and entrepreneurial spirit through starting LGBTQ meet-ups and YouTube video blog.
- Creative risk taker, not afraid to speak out about his personal transformation to help others and share his story.

Narrowing Down Possible Topics

Experience: Kaden's Major Experiences and Their Impacts
- **Interning on Hillary Clinton's campaign** (first foray into excitement of politics). Kaden recalled vividly the excitement of working on this campaign and how much he enjoyed being part of the process and supporting a candidate in whom he believed. He also learned how important appearances are in politics and realized that once he came out as a transgender person, he would have to find another medium to effect change because he no longer felt accepted in this world.
- **Filmmaking** (found another vehicle to impact the world). Kaden's experience interning with the NYU graduate film student making

the documentary on transgender teens opened up a new means of expression for Kaden. He discovered a new passion and a world that would accept him as he was. It also prompted him to create a YouTube video blog chronicling his transformation.

- **Performing as a street musician in New York City** (discovered a way to make money through his music and introduced him to an interesting lifestyle and population). Kaden worked as a street musician for a year while he was in community college. He enjoyed the experience immensely and became part of an eclectic, open, and accepting community during a tumultuous time in his life. This experience helped him accept himself and others.

Issue: Personal, Local, National, or International Issue and Its Importance to Kaden

- **LGBTQ rights** (created an open environment for LGBTQ teens to come together). Kaden wanted other teens in his situation to have a place to be themselves without judgment. He started local meet-ups, and, as a result, he became an agent of change for himself and others.

Person: Individuals Who Have Had a Significant Impact on Kaden's Life and Outlook

- **NYU film student.** She took Kaden under her wing and showed him how to use film as a vehicle for effecting change. Based on their experience working together, Kaden developed a new passion and life purpose.
- **YouTube supporters.** Kaden had thousands of supporters who watched his videos and cheered him on during his transformation. These supporters helped him realize his strength and accepted him for who he is. It made him realize how important his work and voice were to the world.

■ ■ ■ Possible Essay Topic Summary Chart ■ ■ ■

Experience and Its Impact
Interning on Hillary Clinton's campaign
Ignited his passion for politics and working with others to effect change
Interning with NYU film student on documentary about transgender teens
Identified a new vehicle for change; helped him rediscover his voice
Street musician in Manhattan
Discovered an accepting community during a time when he needed one
Issue and Its Importance
LGBTQ rights
Importance of providing a safe haven for teens, run by teens
Person and His or Her Impact
NYU film student
Showed him another path to expression and how he could make a difference in the world outside of politics
YouTube supporters
Gave him a community that accepted and supported him during his transformation

The Personal Statement Essay

Transfer students must identify in their essay why they want to transfer; Kaden's reasons were clear. In his essay, Kaden started off talking about his fascination with politics and his experience working on the Hillary Clinton campaign. He juxtaposed the excitement of the campaign trail with the realization that politics was all about appearances and, given his own transformation, he did not have a place.

The new comfort I had with myself in terms of my political knowledge and capacities gave me enough confidence to come out as transgender. Though my office was very accepting, I soon learned that in politics image is everything, and an image of a gender-bending teenager was not acceptable. When I was sixteen the pressure became too intense. I "came out" to my colleagues as being transgender and left politics shortly thereafter.

Kaden segued into why he developed an interest in film.

Soon after I revealed my true identity to my colleagues, a friend of mine told me about a casting call for transgender teenagers for a Columbia University graduate student short film. Despite my lack of acting skills, I somehow made it to several callback auditions. My amateur acting did not win the role, but through the process I became good friends with the director, who became my mentor in film. Simultaneously I started to document my transition from female to male by making short videos and posting them on YouTube. My inbox is constantly flooded with supporting messages and questions. Seeing the emotional impact that the film and my YouTube videos have had on other people made me realize that the proper medium for me to change the world is not through politics, but through film.

Kaden made a compelling case for why he wanted to transfer and how he would contribute to a film school community. He also included a link to his YouTube video blog as an example of his work.

The Short Answer

After using the personal statement essay to describe his journey to self and ultimately to film, he decided to focus his short answer on his leadership and entrepreneurial skills. He described the impetus for starting the LGBTQ meet-ups: a safe haven for teens run by teens free from adult control.

> When I was in high school, I attended three different LGBTQ youth groups where we were confined to a small room and asked to talk about our feelings. These groups felt more like a drug addict support group than anything catered toward teenagers.

He continued to describe how he was able to leverage his Internet popularity to publicize these meet-ups and create a successful experience for LGBTQ teens.

Supplemental Essays by School

None of the schools Kaden applied to required a supplemental essay.

Complementary Angles

Letters of Recommendation

- Kaden asked his teachers from Union County College to write him a letter of recommendation.
- Kaden also got a supplementary letter of recommendation from the NYU film student director. She was able to speak to Kaden's filmmaking talents.

Brag Sheet/Resume

- Kaden focused on the details of his film experience, his leadership setting up LGBTQ meet-ups, his political campaign work, and his musical talent and experience. In his main personal statement and short answer he discussed why he pursued these activities, and the brag sheet was able to showcase the extent of his activities in more detail. He also included a link to his YouTube video blog.

Supplemental Materials/Audition

- Kaden submitted a portfolio of his film work.

Additional Information

- Kaden described why he did not do as well during his high school career and that he needed to stay home to help his family while his father was undergoing cancer treatment. He uploaded his detailed brag sheet/resume here.

Results

Kaden applied and was accepted to SUNY Purchase film school. He decided not to apply anywhere else because after his visit he felt very comfortable and he knew that they had an excellent yet affordable program. He also liked that he could have a transgender roommate to ease his transition.

Final Decision

SUNY Purchase

What Can You Learn from Kaden's Story?
Questions to Ask Yourself

- Does your academic record accurately reflect your potential? Why or why not? What is getting in the way of you succeeding academically? Do you need to take some time off to regroup and figure out a new direction?
- Have you changed directions in your academic interests? Does the college you are currently attending still meet your needs? If not, what type of school do you need? How can you get there? What are your reasons for wanting to change, and how can you articulate them clearly to an admissions committee?
- What personal issues are you dealing with? How have you overcome them? What did you learn from these challenges? How have you grown as a result of overcoming these challenges?
- What risks have you taken in your life? How did they turn out for you? Did they seem like risks at the time or just something that you needed to do? How has your idea of risk changed since you took the first one?

- What talents do you have that can help you offset a shaky academic record?

Notes

JENNY
THE RESERVED
NATURAL ATHLETE

Jenny's Snapshot

- GPA: 3.6 (weighted, out of 4.2)
- Rigor: 8 AP/honors classes
- SAT: 1100/1710
- ACT with writing: N/A
- Class rank: 25/103 (top 25 percent)

About Jenny

- Main interests: basketball, volleyball, team sports
- Jenny was a natural athlete and six feet tall. She excelled at every sport she tried.
- Jenny started on the varsity basketball team as a freshman at a large suburban high school and continued on the varsity team after transferring to a small Catholic high school her sophomore year. Jenny also played AAU club basketball throughout high

school. As a sophomore, she received an NJAC Honorable Mention All-Conference, and as a junior, she made Second Team All-Conference.

- Jenny also played varsity volleyball at her high school from sophomore through senior year. During her sophomore year, she was named offensive MVP and was also named to the NJAC All-Academic Team and NJAC First Team All-Conference. She was named to the NJAC Second Team All-Conference her junior year.

- Jenny was a respected athlete and team member at her school. She was on the reserved and quiet side, but used sports as a springboard to develop her confidence, interpersonal skills, and leadership by becoming captain for the varsity basketball and volleyball teams.

- Jenny displayed a strong interest in working with children, acting as a counselor at a girls' basketball camp, a volunteer counselor at a summer playground camp, and a volunteer counselor at her local YMCA. She also volunteered at fund-raisers to assist abused and battered children.

- Jenny was selected by her teachers and school ministry to serve as a peer leader for her classmates.

- Jenny liked science and was thinking that she might like to pursue a career in physical therapy, kinesiology, or athletic training. She also wanted to play on the basketball team in college.

Personality Profile

Jenny came across as a reserved, quiet young lady. Her parents divorced when she was in third grade, and there was a good deal of tension in her home stemming from the divorce. She was not comfortable speaking about her problems with her friends or her family, and kept her feelings bottled up inside.

As a freshman, she initially played varsity soccer at a large suburban high school, and felt uncomfortable around the other team members. She felt they ostracized her and resented her for playing varsity as a freshman. She found herself releasing her frustration about her family and team situations through aggressive playing on the soccer field. Realizing that the situation with her soccer team was not emotionally healthy for her, Jenny quit the team after its third practice. She tried out for the volleyball team and immediately made varsity despite her lack of experience. The girls on the volleyball team made her feel welcome, and she realized that positive change can be achieved by taking action to eliminate a bad situation.

Despite the support that Jenny felt from her new teammates, she still felt that the large high school was not the appropriate forum for her to grow as a person. She began to understand that she would prefer a smaller, more nurturing environment and made the bold move to switch to a small Catholic high school her sophomore year. Her mother encouraged her by telling her that only she could effect her own happiness, and that if she was unhappy it was only because of what she was doing to herself.

After Jenny switched schools, she flourished athletically, socially, and academically. Her confidence grew and she learned to open up to others. She realized that she needed to address the root cause of her anger and anxiety rather than merely acting aggressively on the field.

Academically, Jenny was a strong student in the top quarter of her class. She enjoyed science and math, and contemplated combining those interests with her love of sports. She was considering majors in physical therapy, kinesiology, or athletic training in college.

Although sports took up the majority of Jenny's time, she spent time volunteering for an organization that supports abused and battered children and raising money for her team.

Jenny wanted to play basketball in college and was deciding whether she would prefer a Division I, II, or III school. Financial aid would factor into her decision, so if she did not get an athletic scholarship, it would be important to get some merit aid or consider state schools (which are typically much larger than Jenny preferred).

Creating Jenny's College Application Wheel

I met Jenny during January of her sophomore year. Her athletic prowess stood out, as she was already a starting player on her high school's varsity basketball and volleyball teams. She also played for a competitive basketball club team. We both knew that Jenny would play the athletic angle; the question was, at what level? Did she want to be an athlete first and student second and pursue Division I or II sports, or did she want to be a student first and athlete second and pursue Division III schools? We discussed the difference between the divisions, and I told Jenny to think about the various options and determine what made the most sense for her. She would need to start reaching out to coaches by the end of the year by sending them a copy of her athletic resume and tapes, as well as letting them know which showcases she would be playing. Finally, we had to identify some summer college basketball camps that would put her in front of coaches of interest.

Given Jenny's value to the team, I suggested that she develop her leadership skills by trying to become captain of at least one of the teams on which she played. I also suggested that she work with her club basketball coach to identify basketball teams that would be a good fit for her at the college level. While Jenny excelled at both sports, she had been getting more interest from college basketball coaches, so we felt that basketball would be her best bet. Yet, if she decided to pursue Division III schools, she could also play the dual sport angle.

Academically, Jenny was doing well, but she tended to have a more difficult time with history tests that covered a lot of material. We discussed some study techniques, such as making flash cards, to help her remember more material during history tests. Jenny had a natural ability and interest in math and science and enjoyed English, so she challenged herself in those subjects. During her junior year she took honors physics, marine science, AP statistics, honors English, US history, and theology. She dropped foreign language after sophomore year since that was more of a challenge for her.

During this initial meeting, Jenny expressed an interest in science and animals and thought she might want to be a veterinarian. We discussed exploring a pre-college veterinary program or getting an internship at the pharmaceutical company where her mom worked to learn more about these fields.

Jenny had done some community service by volunteering for a home for battered women and doing several basketball fundraisers. We brainstormed some ideas for her to go deeper in community service during the spring and summer when she was less busy with her sports. She seemed interested in volunteering at her local YMCA in the childcare center as well as becoming a peer minister in her school during her senior year. These two activities would also strengthen her leadership.

Jenny's Strengths
- Athletic excellence in basketball and volleyball
- Overcame adversity and made a positive change in her life
- Opportunity to become a leader in multiple areas
- Ability to manage challenging schedule and two sports
- Solid student, top quarter of the class academically
- Hardworking and motivated
- Strong in math and science

Jenny's Weaknesses
- Difficulty with testing could become a problem for standardized tests
- Could tend toward a lack of confidence; needed a supportive, nurturing environment
- Limited time to pursue community service or other non-sports-related activities

Jenny's Checklist

Jenny was performing well on her basketball team and needed to continue to do so while maintaining her A/B average, with an effort to lean more toward A's than B's in the majority of her courses. She needed to find the time to prepare for her SATs or ACTs, despite her heavy sports involvement. She would achieve this by obtaining some private test prep tutoring.

Jenny also needed to reach out to schools of interest to her and maintain contact with coaches. She needed to reach out to her own coaches to help her with this process. Jenny also needed to schedule official school visits (when invited) to determine not only the match with the school but also the match with the team. As her sports team would become her predominant community in college, it was important that she feel comfortable with the team. I advised her to follow up with coaches who contacted her via email to express interest and start building relationships. (Division I coaches cannot communicate by phone with students before July 1 of their senior year of high school; however, email and texting are acceptable.)

In her free time, Jenny needed to continue to round out her profile by demonstrating interest in service to the community and to her school. She also needed to think about what was important to her in a college community, since it has always been important to her to feel welcomed and comfortable in a group environment.

I suggested that Jenny should strive to become captain of at least her basketball team her senior year, to demonstrate her leadership skills and to show that she had earned the respect of her peers and her coaches.

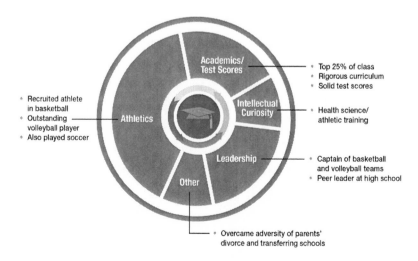

Jenny's Application Wheel: Fall of Senior Year

- **Academics:** Jenny had a solid academic record with an A/B average. Her grades had shown improvement since freshman year, especially after she transferred schools and gained more confidence, and she needed to continue to push to show that upward trend. I advised Jenny to continue to take science and math courses at the honors and AP level, when possible, but realistically balance what she could handle while also playing varsity and club sports.

- **Test scores:** Jenny scored a 1740 on her SATs, with a 530 in critical reading, a 600 in math, and a 610 in writing. Jenny could opt to take the test again to try to hit the 600 range in critical reading. She needed to decide if she would have time to study for another sitting of the test versus channeling more of her time into her sports. Her scores would become more critical if she chose a college at which she was not being recruited for basketball. Jenny did not need to take any SAT subject tests for the schools to which she was applying. She could also consider test-optional schools.

- **Athletics:** This was a key piece of Jenny's chart. She needed to continue to strive for excellence in basketball and showcase her talent to coaches at AAU tournaments. She had to continue to communicate with coaches and keep them up to date on her accomplishments.

- **Special talent:** Jenny's special talent was her athleticism.

- **Intellectual curiosity:** Jenny was interested in science and needed to continue to demonstrate this interest by taking classes in that area. Jenny expressed an interest in pursuing an athletic training or physical therapy career, and although she did not have the time to intern in these fields, she showed some connection to athletic training in her work with children at sports camps. Outside of this area, Jenny had not demonstrated any strong intellectual curiosity in a particular field.

- **Leadership:** Jenny showed her leadership capabilities by being selected as captain of both her basketball and volleyball teams. She also showed leadership skills by being selected as a peer leader by the faculty and clergy at her school.

- **Other:** Jenny overcame adversity by recognizing that she controls her own destiny. This would be important to communicate to schools as it showed her resilience and strength of character.
- **Financial:** Finances were an issue for Jenny's family, and financial aid would impact where she went to school. As a result, Jenny needed to consider merit and athletic scholarships as well as any financial aid package that she was offered.

Developing the College List

The process of developing a college list for an athlete varies slightly from that for a non-athlete because the list can fluctuate dramatically depending on which school is doing the courting. The challenge for a recruited athlete is to get the athletic, academic, and social fits to align.

Early on in the process, Jenny was recruited by several Division I schools, including Marist College. Marist's coach had seen Jenny play at various AAU tournaments. Jenny was not ready to commit so early, and by the time she got back to the coach, the coach had already filled her roster. Each week Jenny informed me of various coaches who contacted her and invited her for an official visit with the team. (An official visit is when the coach invites you to meet the team and visit the school. You cannot be considered a recruited athlete without this official visit.) While visiting schools, Jenny asked the following questions of the coaches:

- What is it like being a scholar-athlete here?
- What sort of advising is there for pre-health sciences, physical therapy, and education?
- What did you like best about your experience here? (if appropriate)
- What type of student does well here?
- What's the transition like for students here from high school to college?
- What sort of community service projects are there for students?

Although Jenny was heavily recruited initially, interest from Division I coaches began to dwindle by the middle of junior year. Jenny had also evolved her thinking with regard to basketball and her major. She decided that she wanted to be a student first and an athlete second, and therefore pursue Division III basketball. Her interest in science remained; however, she now wanted a career that would combine this interest with her talent for sports. She identified several pre-health majors, including physical therapy, kinesiology, sports medicine, and athletic training, that would marry her interests and abilities. She also considered biology as another pathway to achieve her goals since many of the schools that expressed an interest in her playing basketball did not offer the pre-health majors.

Socially, it was important for Jenny to feel comfortable on the campuses on her list. She had already experienced the feeling of being different or left out during her freshman year at the large suburban public high school, and she understood how she had thrived when she switched to a small private high school where she felt accepted and welcomed. This feeling of inclusion would be vital to Jenny's success at college, and the vibe she got from the team and the student body would therefore be critical to her decision.

Jenny was also looking for financial aid in the form of merit and athletic money, and she would therefore look for schools that offered the most generous packages.

Key College Criteria for Jenny

- A small to medium school with no more than 15,000 students; ideal size would be 4,000 to 5,000 students
- A college that offers a pre-health track, but open to either a pre-professional or liberal arts environment
- Strong Division III basketball team, but would consider playing at the club level for some Division I or II schools
- Structured curriculum with easy access to professors and the opportunity to participate in small class discussions
- A more studious environment, with a down-to-earth culture and a liberal political bent.
- No preference for an urban, suburban, rural, or outdoorsy campus; however, she preferred to be within a four-hour drive from home

- A coed environment; open to a Catholic school
- Brand name of the school was not important
- Financial aid definitely a factor

The Final List

The Reaches

- **University of Rochester:** The basketball coach was extremely interested in Jenny for the team. While it has strong science programs, Jenny would not be able to pursue kinesiology or athletic training and overall did not feel like it was the best fit.
- **Trinity College:** Jenny was actively recruited by the basketball coach, but unfortunately Jenny did not feel like the team or culture was a good fit for her.

The Possibles

- **University of Delaware:** Jenny liked the campus. It has a good physical therapy/pre-health program, and her sister was there and loved the school. Jenny would be willing to forego basketball to go here.
- **The College of New Jersey:** TCNJ has strong pre-health programs and good Division III sports. The price was also favorable given that it is a public school.

The Likelies

- **Dickinson College:** Jenny liked the size, and the coach was interested. She would have to major in biology since they do not offer athletic training or kinesiology.
- **Ithaca College:** The accelerated physical therapy program appealed to Jenny, and the coach expressed interest in her.
- **Marist College:** Marist's coach had expressed interest in Jenny early on, but she ultimately filled her team before Jenny was willing to commit. It had a lot of positive aspects for Jenny, including a beautiful campus, compatible academic offerings,

strong sports teams, and good interaction between faculty and students; however, she would not be able to play basketball.

- **Ursinus College:** The coach was very interested in Jenny, and she went on an official visit. She felt very comfortable with the team, and the strong science facilities and faculty impressed her. Even though Ursinus is a liberal arts college, it offers exercise and sports science as a major, which was perfect for Jenny's interests.

The Safety

- **University of Scranton:** It has the majors that she wanted and Jenny felt comfortable with the environment. The basketball coach was also interested in her.

Choosing an Essay Topic

After brainstorming with Jenny about experiences that affected her most, we identified several themes that she wanted to communicate within her application.

- Dealing with the pressure of playing three varsity sports and balancing schoolwork made her realize how important it is to rely on herself and work on her own.

- If she was upset about something, taking it out on the sports field only hurt herself and her teammates. It was important to control her aggression and anger by communicating her hurt to someone rather than becoming sullen and aggressive.

- When she realized that she didn't fit in at the large suburban high school, she knew that she needed to make a change. Her mother reinforced this idea, and taught her that she needed to take control of her own life and that only she could be responsible for her own happiness or unhappiness.

- When she started playing volleyball, she found true friends who supported her and appreciated her talent. This enabled her to get her emotions in check and start confiding in others.

- Suffering in silence is never the answer to a problem. Jenny was unhappy as a result of her parents' divorce, pressure and jealousy from teammates, the pressures of school, and an unsatisfying social life. By changing schools and feeling more accepted, Jenny learned to open up to others, share her feelings, and, as a result, become much happier and more successful academically, socially, and athletically.

- Sports have always been an outlet for her, but she has learned to broaden her outlets through friends, family, and spirituality.

Narrowing Down Possible Topics

Experience: Jenny's Major Experiences and Their Impacts

- **Jenny's parents' divorce left her feeling angry and confused.** This, combined with her feelings of ostracism and stress as she began high school, left Jenny feeling sullen. She bottled this up inside and took her aggressions out on the soccer field (Jenny played soccer during her freshman year). With her mother's guidance, she took control of her own life by switching schools and finding an environment that was more suited to her. As she made friends and gained acceptance, she found herself better able to open up to her friends and family, and she began to thrive. She learned that the best way to confront obstacles is directly and honestly, and that it is not healthy to keep things bottled up inside.

- **When Jenny sprained her ankle, she was out of sports for six weeks.** She realized that she'd have to work twice as hard as before to compensate, and she was determined to do that. She realized how hard she had worked to get where she was and how one small thing could destroy that. She realized that she should not take anything for granted, because you never know when it can be taken away. Jenny was determined to overcome this setback. This determination was what would make her a success in college as well.

- **Jenny went on a weekend retreat with her school to learn about God.** This helped her develop a relationship with God and was a religious awakening for her. The small groups of students discussed a variety of topics in a nonjudgmental environment, and the weekend was very meaningful for Jenny.

Person: Individuals Who Have Had a Significant Impact on Jenny's Life and Outlook

- **Her mom.** Jenny's mom is always the first person to whom she will go to talk. Her mother is the one who taught her to take responsibility for her own happiness and to change things that make her unhappy. After the divorce, Jenny's dad was absent from her life, and her mother took on the sole parenting role. Jenny's mom was always willing to help her with anything, and could always be trusted.
- **Friends.** Jenny learned to turn to her friends for support and advice. Friends go through the same things as she does: sports, boys, family. She learned that when she could commiserate with others, it made her feel that she was not alone.

■ ■ ■ Possible Essay Topic Summary Chart ■ ■ ■

Experience and Its Impact
Dealing in silence with her frustration of feeling ostracized by her team and parents' divorce.
Forced Jenny to confront what would make her happy and led to her transferring schools; there she was accepted and learned the value of opening up to others
Ability on the athletic field
Taught her the importance of being versatile and determined
Issue and Its Importance
Effecting positive change to better one's situation
Saw improvement in every aspect of her life once she took action to change what she did not like

Person and His or Her Impact
Mother Taught her that she was responsible for her own happiness or unhappiness and needed to take control of her own life
Teammates Importance of working together as a team

The Personal Statement Essay

Jenny felt that the most transformative experience for her in high school was acknowledging her unhappiness and addressing it by transferring schools. That enabled her to form stronger friendships, become part of a team that was a comfortable fit for her, and gain more confidence in all areas of her life. She also wanted to show how her personal tendency toward shyness and distrust of others was transformed on the basketball and volleyball courts, where she had to be part of a team and be aggressive to win the game. She also wanted to convey to the reader that the sports venue really was her home.

> When I was younger, I lived behind a wall of silence and sports. My parents divorced when I was in third grade, and after that I was afraid to open up to my family. I felt that all of my problems were minor compared to everything that was going on, so I kept all my feelings inside. I was also very shy and quiet, so I never really felt comfortable trusting and opening up to others outside of my family. At the time, I accepted my unhappiness and I thought I was alone and preferred to suffer in silence. However, there was one place that I found relaxation: playing sports.

Jenny described how she reached a point where she did not want to suffer in silence anymore. She reached out to her mom, who helped her to realize that only she could change her situation. Jenny poignantly shows how, by finally reaching out, she could see how her mother was there for her completely and how opening up could improve her life.

> I decided it was time to break the silence and share what I had been feeling with my mom. All of my feelings that were building up from the divorce on, whether it was my social life, friends isolating me, or pressures of school, just exploded. My mom comforted me and helped me realize that feeling better and being happy were in my control. I convinced my mom to let me take a risk and transfer to a new school.

Jenny went on to explain how the new school helped her to develop into a happier, more confident person. She also showed how her intellectual interest developed there and her social interactions improved.

> There were smaller classes with teachers that only aimed to help students, and my academics became stronger than they were my freshman year. I was able to take more challenging classes that I thought I would not be able to take, and I developed a strong interest in the sciences. I then pursued that interest and began shadowing my athletic trainer in the spring. There were also new groups of people that I could interact with and become friends with, and new sports teams that I could play on. I realized that I thrived in a smaller, more nurturing environment.

Jenny concluded by showing the growth she achieved personally and academically as a result of taking a risk and changing schools.

> I began to speak up and open up to others about what I thought. I found that the more I shared, the more confident I became. I finally felt like I fit in.

The topic discussed by Jenny could address the prompt "Describe a place or environment where you are perfectly content. What do you do or experience there, and why is it meaningful to you?" Jenny showed that the environment in which she was most comfortable was on the basketball court or sports field, but that she was also comfortable in a small, nurturing, supportive environment. By affirmatively choosing an environment that could help Jenny grow, she was able to better show her leadership on the sports field, her athleticism, and the development of her intellectual curiosity to combine her love of science and sports.

The Short Answer

Jenny conveyed the intensity of her involvement on the basketball court in a way that reiterated her love of sport and her commitment and determination in a game. This juxtaposed her confident side with the more fragile, tentative part of her personality that she revealed in her main essay.

> I entered the second half of the county championships with four fouls. With five minutes remaining, my goal was to stay composed on defense, drive in and score on offense, and shoot a couple outside shots throughout the game, and make them. My versatility with the ball made me unpredictable. There were two minutes left. My teammate drove in, got fouled, but missed the foul shot. The game was tied. I got the rebound off of the foul shot, kicked it out, got the ball back, and drove past my defender, who was not expecting me to drive. I scored, winning us the county championships.

Jenny's short answer did more than show her scoring the winning shot in the game, which can be a trite and overused theme. In this short answer, the focus was more on Jenny's versatility, confidence, judgment, and leadership on the field. As an applicant striving to be a recruited athlete, Jenny would be untrue to herself not to write about the impact sports have on her life.

Supplemental Essays by School

Because Jenny was recruited prior to having to submit other applications, she did not prepare any supplemental essays. However, in anticipating the question "Why this school?" Jenny's key points would have been to focus on her feeling of "fit" with the basketball team and the presence of a major that worked with her interests in physical therapy, kinesiology, and athletic training.

Complementary Angles

Letters of Recommendation

- Jenny asked her honors physics teacher, who could speak to her interest in science, and her English teacher, who could address her writing skills, for letters of recommendation.
- She got a supplemental letter from her athletic trainer to speak to her leadership on the team and her determination and persistence on the field.
- For schools where she was interested in playing basketball, she also got a letter from her AAU basketball team coach.

Brag Sheet/Resume

During her junior year, Jenny prepared a single-page athletic profile that she sent out to coaches. She had her photograph on the top, so that coaches would be able to easily identify her at tournaments. There was also a very brief mention of her academic achievements and her community service activities, followed by a fuller description of her basketball accomplishments. She included her coach's name and contact information, positions she played, her team's achievements, and her individual achievements as well as information on her AAU team, including positions she played and her individual achievements and stats. She also added a few lines at the bottom regarding her individual achievements on the varsity volleyball team.

For her applications, Jenny prepared a simple two-page brag sheet. The majority of the first page outlined her athletic activities: teams on which she played, the hours involved, and her positions and honors relating to the teams. She then briefly described her summer work experiences, her community service work, and other extracurricular activities. She ended by describing her academic awards and honors.

Supplemental Materials
- The letter to the coaches was the most important supplemental piece of Jenny's wheel. She also sent a tape to several schools to garner interest in coming to tournaments to see her play.
- Jenny also communicated with coaches from several schools during junior year and early fall of senior year. She maintained consistent communication and continued to update them throughout the year.
- She also conducted several official visits to meet with the team and coaches.

Additional Information
Jenny did not have any extenuating circumstances to report in her record. She uploaded her brag sheet here.

Results
Jenny submitted applications to only some of the schools on her original list.

The Possibles
- **University of Delaware:** Withdrew
- **The College of New Jersey:** Withdrew

The Likelies
- **Dickinson College:** Withdrew
- **Marist College:** Withdrew
- **Ursinus College:** Accepted early decision

The Safety
- **University of Scranton:** Withdrew

Final Decision

After being recruited by Ursinus College in the fall of her senior year, Jenny committed to the team and applied early decision. In the end, Jenny's decision was easy because Ursinus met all of her criteria: a small, nurturing environment; excellent sciences as well as an exercise science major; a tight-knit basketball team; and enough merit money to make it affordable. Upon her acceptance to Ursinus, she withdrew her applications from the other schools.

What Can You Learn from Jenny's Story? Questions to Ask Yourself

- If you are an athlete, are you interested in playing that team sport in college? How intense do you want that experience to be—that is, would you prefer a Division I, II, or III school? Would you prefer to play a club sport?

- Are you committed to a particular academic field? How does that commitment compare to your commitment to play your sport? Which is the greater priority for you?

- Have you ever been in a situation that has overwhelmed you and made you unhappy? What did you do to change that experience? Could you have taken more positive action to improve your situation? If you did take action, how did that make you feel? Is the situation resolved?

- What kind of learning experience has worked best for you? Do you thrive in smaller classes in which you can get to know the teacher personally and develop a relationship? Do you prefer larger classes that are more lecture oriented? Should or will this affect the size and type of college that you seek out?

- If you are an athlete, will you be happy at the school you choose if athletics is no longer part of the equation?

Notes

8

ADAM
THE SUPER
SCIENCE NERD

Lessons Learned during the Application Process

Adam's case will demonstrate several important lessons. The first is how to use an incredible strength to compensate for a weakness and how to turn a blip in your record into something positive. The second is how important it is to take leaps of faith to follow your passions. The final lesson is how to showcase your scientific research.

Adam's Snapshot

- GPA: 3.7 (weighted, out of 4.4)
- Rigor: 9 AP/honors classes
- SAT: 1390/2040
- ACT with writing: 33
- SAT subject tests: biology: 710; chemistry: 740; math 2: 800
- Class rank: top 50 percent

About Adam

- Main interests: science, math, physics, economics, philosophy
- Adam was highly gifted in math and science. He struggled with language-based subjects such as English and history, but he loved to learn. He actively engaged in the classroom, participated in online math competitions, and read science and philosophy books and articles for fun.
- He was involved in his high school's independent science research program, which allows students to conduct their own science research project during high school.
- He spent the summer between junior and senior year conducting research at a lab in Greece. This opportunity not only exposed him to new cultures, but also allowed him to recognize how well he fit into a scientific community. He was also cited in a scientific article and used his research to become a semifinalist in the Siemens Competition in Math, Science, and Technology.
- Adam had ADHD as well as a learning difference that made it difficult for him to read and process language efficiently. He suffered some health issues during his sophomore year, which impacted his ability to take his ADHD medication and caused him to perform below his usual standards during his sophomore year.
- Adam was very active in his temple and shared his passion for Judaism with elementary students in his temple's religious school.
- Adam was the oldest of three children, but luckily financial aid would not impact where he went to school.

Personality Profile

Adam was feisty and quirky; he had very strong opinions and was deeply passionate about his interests and sharing them (even when not asked). Math, science, and Judaism were the three areas of his life that most closely defined him. He started in his high school's science research program as a sophomore, which provided him with an outlet to develop his natural strengths. Adam enjoyed participating in various online math competitions. He also took great pleasure in getting younger kids excited about Jewish history and culture by teaching in his temple's religious school.

While Adam was gifted in science and math, he struggled with language and organizational skills. He had attention deficit/hyperactivity disorder (ADHD), which he was able to manage fairly well with medication. But during the early part of high school, Adam was not very motivated. His natural intelligence allowed him to get by with B's and B+'s without having to do a lot of outside work. That all changed during sophomore year, when he developed an illness that prevented him from taking his ADHD medication. Suddenly, Adam had to work twice as hard to maintain his B's and B+'s. He became frustrated and felt defeated. Even though he was working twice as hard, his grades were not better. Once he recovered and was able to go back on his ADHD medication, Adam had an epiphany. He realized that he had been squandering his God-given gift of intelligence and that it was not enough to be smart; he had to work hard to achieve greatness. He came back to school his junior year with a renewed sense of purpose and interest in learning.

Creating Adam's College Application Wheel

I met Adam during the spring of his sophomore year. During our first meeting, we discussed Adam's interest in science and we talked about some ways that he could pursue research. He questioned my knowledge about scientific research and whether or not I was in a position to give him advice on this topic. As a sophomore in high school, Adam was clearly at a higher level than me scientifically, so he was right to question my scientific prowess. So I reassured him that my experience mentoring other budding scientists along with what I learned through my husband's experience as a physician scientist mentoring young scientists for the past fifteen years could be helpful to him.

Of immediate concern were his grades. He had a mix of A's and B's during his freshman year, but mostly B's and B−'s during his sophomore year. I could tell that he was extremely intelligent in math and science by the way he spoke. But I also knew that intellectual curiosity would not be enough to help him reach his goal of attending a highly select science-focused university if he did not have good grades. He assured me that his past performance was due to his illness during sophomore year and that junior year would be different. We created a plan for him to focus on improving his grades, go deep in his science research by finding a mentor who could work with him the following summer and prepare him to enter the Siemens Competition, and continue to build leadership by teaching at his temple's Hebrew school.

We met again in November of his junior year. Adam greeted me with a twinkle in his eye and seemed much happier and more confident. He said, "I think you'll be happy with my progress." He laid out his report card with great flourish on the table. Every single class had an A next to it. He beamed. And so did I. When he left the previous year I knew how difficult it would be to improve his grades so dramatically; I was thrilled with his turnaround. "This is amazing, Adam. What did you do differently?" I asked. "Well, once I was able to take my medication again and focus, I put that same energy into my work as I had without the medication, but now I could actually get results." So now that Adam had been able to get his grades up to his potential, we needed to focus on the rest of his profile.

Adam felt more comfortable with the SAT, so he focused his test prep there. I suggested that he start visiting schools and keep a journal to keep track of what he liked and did not like at various schools to help me narrow down his list. He was going to continue working at his temple's Hebrew school and participating in online math competitions, but the biggest challenge for him was identifying a summer research opportunity. As part of the independent science research program at his high school, Adam had to find a mentor to let him work in a lab so he could pursue his research. We brainstormed on some local medical schools that provided high school science opportunities, and he was also going to ask his high school science advisor.

Adam's Strengths

- Exceptional math and science student
- Highly motivated after his illness and renewed sense of purpose
- Improved grades junior year
- Highly intellectually curious
- Would be a contender in Siemens Competition and had depth of science unparalleled by many high school students
- Ability to overcome adversity and grow from it
- Strong understanding of strengths and weaknesses

Adam's Weaknesses

- Sophomore year grades did not reflect his potential
- Difficulty with English and heavily reading-based subjects
- Poor organizational skills
- Learning difference (but that is becoming much less of a weakness)

Adam's Checklist

Adam had a mixed academic record, but his turnaround junior year was impressive. His goal was to continue with strong grades and build depth in his strengths of math and science. With his newfound work ethic, Adam would be able to study for the SAT and get close to an 800 in the math section and mid to high 600s in the critical reading and writing sections. I advised him that he should also be open to taking the ACT, because strong math and science students often perform better on them.

Adam needed to find a summer research opportunity to complete his independent science research program and prepare for the

Siemens Competition. He had a clear math and science angle, and this opportunity would sharpen that angle and start him on his path to becoming a scientific researcher. He also needed to round out his angle through his passion for Judaism and teaching in his temple's religious school.

Adam pursued various leads to identify a summer research opportunity. He had contacted a professor at the University of Pennsylvania who was working on a similar line of research. She responded to him with interest. Adam was ecstatic. But the only problem was that she was no longer at the University of Pennsylvania; she had moved back to Greece and invited Adam to spend the summer at her lab in Athens. He called me and asked me what I thought: Should he do it? His mom was a little nervous but not opposed to the idea. I replied, "Absolutely! This is an amazing opportunity for you on so many levels." So Adam accepted and spent the summer in a lab in Greece pursuing his research. It ended up being a life-changing experience in more ways than just scientifically.

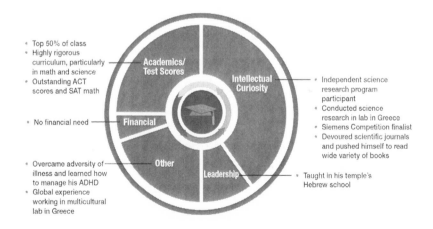

Adam's Application Wheel: Fall of Senior Year

- **Academics:** Adam maintained straight A's his junior year and continued with a stellar record into senior year. He challenged himself in his areas of strength by taking four higher-level math and science classes, including AP calculus BC (the higher level), advanced physics, computer science 2, and his independent science research class. He dropped social studies, but maintained Latin 4 and English 4.

- **Test scores:** Adam reached his goal in the SAT but decided to try the ACT as well. Overall, he did better on the ACT, with a composite score of 33 (he received the highest score possible of a 36 in the math and science sections). He also took three SAT subject tests, including math 2, biology, and chemistry, which he needed to apply to Johns Hopkins University.
- **Athletics:** This was not a piece of Adam's wheel.
- **Special talent:** Adam had a special talent for numbers and quantitative science. He showed this through participating in math contests and the type of scientific research he did.
- **Intellectual curiosity:** Adam exuded intellectual curiosity through his fascination with science, mathematics, philosophy, and Judaism. Even though reading was at times a challenge, he devoured scientific journals and books about science. Adam loved talking about science with other scientists, which he discovered while working in a lab in Greece.
- **Leadership:** Adam displayed leadership through his job teaching in his temple's Hebrew school and also through his independent science research project. In both instances he got others excited about his passions.
- **Other:** Adam overcame adversity through his illness sophomore year. He showed great strength of character by learning that he had previously been squandering his gifts by not working to his full capacity. His renewed sense of purpose and drive would make him an attractive candidate for a college.
- **Financial:** Adam did not have financial need.

Developing the College List

Adam wanted a liberal arts curriculum with a very strong science program. His academic interests included physics, math, philosophy, and economics. He wanted the ability to form strong relationships with his professors, ample opportunity to pursue his science research, and a diverse environment where he could engage in intellectual discussions similar to what he experienced in the lab in Greece. He was not as concerned about the size of the school as long as he had opportunities to get involved in research. He thought an honors college in a larger school would be a good option as well. He did not want Greek life to dominate the social scene, but he was not opposed to schools with Greek life. He also wanted a strong Jewish life on campus.

Key College Criteria for Adam

- Size of the college was not as important as the opportunity
- Preferred a liberal arts environment with excellent science and research opportunities
- Wanted to study physics, math, economics, and philosophy
- Prestige of the school was less important than the opportunities and fit
- Wanted to have good interaction with faculty and the ability to find like-minded students, particularly in the sciences
- Was prepared to work hard
- Wanted to become active in Hillel (the Jewish organization on campus)
- Wanted an intellectually curious (nerdy okay) student body with varied interests

The Final List

The Reach

- **Massachusetts Institute of Technology:** MIT is one of the top technical institutions in the country. Adam felt he should apply here even though it was not his top choice. He did not feel as comfortable on the MIT campus as at some other colleges.

The Possible
- **Johns Hopkins University:** Adam went crazy over the abundant research opportunities and physics lab. He also felt very comfortable on campus and liked the strong Jewish community.

The Likelies
- **Brandeis University:** Adam liked the programs, atmosphere, and campus feel. He also felt it would be easy to do a double major at Brandeis, and he particularly liked the biological physics major.
- **University of Maryland at College Park:** Adam thought its science honors program would be a good option.
- **University of Rochester:** This was one of Adam's favorite schools. He loved the intellectual, somewhat nerdy feel of the student body. He thought the research opportunities were outstanding and felt that the overall feel of the student body matched his personality well.

The Safeties
- **Rensselaer Polytechnic Institute:** Adam was not as interested in RPI as some of the others, but felt like it had good programs in his area of interest.
- **Rochester Institute of Technology:** Adam liked the program and thought he could get involved in research right away.

Choosing an Essay Topic

After brainstorming with Adam about his strengths and interests, we identified several areas that he wanted to communicate within his application.

- How his experience working in a lab in Greece changed him because it not only exposed him to a variety of cultures but also introduced him to a community of scientists.
- He had a true passion for Judaism and enjoyed getting younger kids excited about it.

his passion for science further by introducing ideas and concepts that fascinated him. They made him want to be part of this type of community forever.

■ ■ ■ Possible Essay Topic Summary Chart ■ ■ ■

Experience and Its Impact

Lab in Greece

Exposed him to what a scientific community felt like; taught him how to organize his work and integrate into a community of scientists

Getting sick sophomore year

Taught him that it is not enough to be smart; he also had to work hard to reach his full potential

Teaching Hebrew school

Found a way to get younger kids excited about Judaism; gave him opportunity to be a leader

Issue and Its Importance

Bullying

Stood up for a friend who was being bullied; realized that nobody has the right to stop another person from expressing himself

Person and His or Her Impact

Science teacher

Helped him develop his love of science; showed him opportunities to excel and helped him prepare for the Siemens Competition

Mentors in Greece Lab

Heightened his love of science; pushed him to study on his own to have the knowledge to communicate with them at a higher level

The Personal Statement Essay

Adam knew that he wanted to show how his experience working in a lab in Greece changed him on multiple levels. He found a place where he felt completely comfortable for the first time, a place where he would not be called to task for asking too many questions, a place where people from all over the world enjoyed debating scientific ideas for fun. Yet since writing was not Adam's strong suit, he didn't know how to approach the essay. So in Adam's shoot-from-the-hip manner, he wrote:

> ...And then my friend, Manos, a PhD candidate for bioinformatics who was frustrated because he had to fix a program he had created, picks a fight with another PhD candidate. I grow excited as he asks the question, knowing that it will be a well fought argument between physics believers and biologists at heart. He asks, "So why does biology not have any equations like physics? Biology needs a Kepler to save it." And so the war begins between issues like complementarity, protein motifs, $F = mA$, etc.

I read through the essay several times to make sure that I was not missing the beginning section. When we met the next week, I asked Adam about it, and he replied, "I didn't know how to start, so I just started in the middle." I smiled because it was so Adam, but it worked.

He went on to let the reader know that he heard this conversation during lunch at the Alexander Fleming Biomedical Sciences Research Center in Greece. This set up that he was doing scientific research in a foreign country, two angles that made him a strong candidate: intellectual curiosity and global experience.

This topic addressed the Common Application prompt "Describe a place or environment where you are perfectly content. What do you do or experience there, and why is it meaningful to you?" Adam showed his deep desire to engage intellectually and how the lab provided him with precisely this type of environment, one he had not previously experienced.

Before my time in the bioinformatics lab, I never imagined how difficult it is to communicate creative ideas because it is not learned during school. In school, other students belittled my ideas because "that's not going to be on the test," but not here. Being part of this scientific community is new to me; it is exciting. It forces me to sort out all of my creative ideas that I have always wanted to explore and explain to others.

Finally, Adam showed that he is not only a bystander, but also a contributor.

I eventually side with Manos and tell him that I think in the future protein and RNA structures will advance to such a level that it will almost be like an equation; he smiles, hinting that he likes my idea a lot.

I look at the clock and notice that the break has sadly come to an end and tell all of my buddies in the lab. We get up and go back upstairs onto the computer to ponder the RNA interactions we are all investigating.

Adam demonstrated his intellectual curiosity as well as his ability to contribute in a meaningful way to a scientific community. He brought the reader right into the conversations that he had while in Greece to illustrate how he would contribute to a college lab community.

The Short Answer

Adam's connection to Judaism was also important to him, and he wanted to talk about his experience teaching in his temple's Hebrew school for the short answer. He focused his essay on the satisfaction he derives from getting kids excited about their faith.

When the kids are running around trying to find all of the mezuzahs or upset because they want to hear more about Mordechai, I know the job is worth it! Knowing that I have helped children get excited about their history makes my Sunday mornings more joyful.

Supplemental Essays by School

Adam had several supplemental essays to write for his list of schools.

- Why this school, and how can you pursue your academic interests here? (Brandeis, Johns Hopkins University, University of Rochester)
- What led to your academic interests? (University of Maryland)
- Do you prefer to go deep in one area or study a wide range of topics and why? (University of Maryland)
- Do you want to do multidisciplinary studies and, if so, what role will you play? (University of Maryland)
- Describe any research you have done. (MIT, University of Rochester)
- Describe your top five activities in more depth. (MIT)
- Describe a setback and what you learned from it. (MIT)

Why This School and How Can You Pursue Your Academic Interests Here?

Adam developed a template for this essay around his desire to do research within the context of a larger liberal arts environment. He described the research that he did in Greece over the summer on microRNAs and identified a professor at each of these schools who could mentor him and allow him to continue his research. This made it easier for him to answer "Why this school?" in a specific way.

After visiting Brandeis I knew that it was a place where I could thrive personally because its overall philosophy of studying liberal arts and sciences for the purpose of bettering oneself strongly matches my own beliefs. However, what really attracted me to Brandeis was the ability to do research in Pengyu Hong's lab. Based on the description of his department on Brandeis' website,

I was excited that Dr. Hong has created a lab that has both computational and laboratory focus, which is really important to what I want to do while at college.

Then he went on to describe the work he did last summer.

I spent last summer conducting research in Dr. H's lab at the Alexander Fleming Institute in Greece. I returned hungry to investigate microRNAs and develop my own line of research.

For schools that asked about academic interests, he began with his lab work description and identified how he could continue this research at a particular school. In each case, Adam made the match between his interest and the school's resources in a very specific way.

Questions 2–4

Adam was able to pull out the section on his academic interests and lab experience to answer each of these questions. For UMD, he talked about his interest in going both deep and broad as a variation of depth in science within the context of a liberal arts environment. He was also able to talk about his interest in multidisciplinary research by bringing in how he looked at the intersection between math and science in his previous work.

Describe Research You Have Done

For this question for the University of Rochester, he was able to describe in great detail the research he did.

I began intensively looking at miRNA features such as linearity of the structures, normalized numbers and unbounded Nucleotides in hairpins, and other known factors. After looking at the histograms of these graphs, the most significant result occurred when I compared the human scoring guide to other species because it supported the idea that the miRNA pathway has changed over time and progressed similarly to evolution.

Top Five Activities

MIT has its own application and does not participate in the Common Application. It asks you to describe your top five activities. Adam listed his independent research on deep sequencing analysis and microRNAs, his math involvement with USA Mathematical Talent Search, his participation in math and science competitions, teaching Hebrew school, and his involvement as a peer-to-peer leader at his high school.

Reaction to a Setback

This question gave Adam the opportunity to discuss his illness during sophomore year and how it opened his eyes to both his strengths and his weaknesses.

> Before getting sick, I had been a smart, if not 100% driven kid. Things had always come easily to me, so I figured that if I could get a B+ without trying or doing the homework, why should I go for the A if it might be an A– no matter how hard I tried? I was a kid who looked for any excuse not to sit down and do my homework and invest myself in studying when I knew I could potentially fail.
>
> Sophomore year was dramatically different. My meds were removed for the first time in over ten years. I felt like a king of spades was removed from my hand of life and replaced with a two of hearts. No matter how hard I tried, my ADHD would find its way to deter me from my goals, and as a result my grades suffered. After two months of unhappiness, I began to formulate a new belief: the idea that maybe grades were not everything and to put forth the effort to learn as much as possible simply to learn.

He continued to describe how he changed and that his illness actually turned out to be a blessing in disguise.

Emotionally, being off my medication made me more vulnerable and depressed in the short term, but it has been more beneficial for the long term by informing me that to be intelligent one needs to be not only smart, but also driven.

This was a heartfelt and honest essay and gave the admissions committees a clear sense of how he had matured and also recovered from setback. It showed that he would be driven to succeed no matter what.

Complementary Angles

Letters of Recommendation

- Adam got letters of recommendation from his math and science teachers.
- He also had two supplemental letters, one from his lab mentor in Greece and one from his boss at his temple. Each one would show a different side of Adam than his teachers could. The science mentor would show his ability to integrate well into a new situation and work collaboratively with other scientists. The Hebrew school supervisor could speak to Adam's success leading younger kids.

Brag Sheet/Resume

- Adam submitted a resume that detailed his scientific accomplishments, including his work in the lab, publications, research experience, and awards, and an abstract of his work. This resume also included his science and math courses and awards and honors in those areas.

Supplemental Materials

- For MIT he included an abstract of the paper he worked on that was published over the summer. He also included the front part of his Siemens Competition application.

Additional Information

- Adam adapted the essay explaining about his illness and its impact on his grades to explain his weaker grades sophomore year. He also included his resume for schools that allowed this additional information.

Results

The Reach

- **Massachusetts Institute of Technology (MIT):** Adam was deferred from his early action application. He accepted this setback as a challenge and wrote MIT a letter explaining why he would be a good fit for the school (even though it was not his first choice). He was ultimately denied.

The Possible

- **Johns Hopkins University:** Accepted

The Likelies

- **Brandeis University:** Accepted with a research stipend of $4,000 per year
- **University of Maryland at College Park:** Accepted into their science scholars program
- **The University of Rochester:** Accepted

The Safeties

- **Rensselaer Polytechnic Institute:** Accepted
- **Rochester Institute of Technology:** Accepted

Final Decision

Johns Hopkins University. The more he learned, the more he realized what an exceptional fit this was for his interests and personality.

What Can You Learn from Adam's Story?
Questions to Ask Yourself

- Have you worked to your full potential? If not, why? What would it take for you to step up your game?

- Are you passionate about a certain subject? Multiple subjects? How have you expressed that?

- Have you overcome a medical condition or other adversity in your life? How did it make you feel? What did you learn from that experience? How have you changed as a result?

- When you are faced with taking a chance, like studying in a foreign country or joining a new situation, how will you respond? What risks have you taken in your life? How have they paid off?

- Have you found a community of people in which you feel totally at home? Why? What about this community makes you feel comfortable? How can you create that environment in college?

- How have you contributed to your religious community or another community? Do you have a passion that you can share with others? How? What can you do?

Notes

9

FRANCESCA
THE CLOSET COMPUTER SCIENCE GIRL AND POPULAR ATHLETE

Lessons Learned during the Application Process

In this case, you will see how Francesca learned to embrace her inner nerd and even convince her friends that programming was cool. Francesca also shows how computer science helped her push beyond her comfort zone academically by forcing her to provide her own sense of structure. Finally, you will see how she got elected captain of the track team through leading by example and cheering on the freshman at every meet.

Francesca's Snapshot

- GPA: 4.36 (weighted, out of 4.38)
- Rigor: 17 AP/honors classes
- SAT: 1550/2350
- ACT with writing: N/A
- SAT subject tests: math 2: 720; physics: 730; chemistry: 680
- Class rank: top 5 percent

About Francesca

- Main interests: computer science, STEM (science, technology, engineering and math) fields
- Francesca was highly intelligent in a quiet, understated way. She thought in code.
- She ran track and cross-country and became captain her senior year by cheering on the underclassmen at every meet.
- She was one of a handful of girls who took wood shop, Visual Basic, AP computer science, and honors computer science 3 during high school.
- Francesca's father was born in Europe, and her mom had Italian roots; she traveled to Europe often to visit her dad's family and had Sunday dinners with her mom's large extended Italian family. Her multicultural upbringing informed her view of the world.
- She emerged as a leader within her school community as a tutor for the National Honor Society, a member of the DREAM Team to educate students about drugs and alcohol, and a transition leader for incoming freshmen.
- She did limited community service through her church.
- Finances would not determine where she goes to school.

Personality Profile

Francesca was an exceptionally strong student challenging herself at the highest level (honors or AP) in all subjects during her sophomore year by taking six academic courses, including Visual Basic as an elective. She thrived with a rigorous schedule and did not shy away from challenge, but also tried to maintain some balance. During her junior year, she took AP or honors-level classes in her five main academic courses with the exception of English and added two more academic electives, AP computer science and AP statistics. During her senior year, she maintained a rigorous curriculum, taking six academic courses with AP calculus BC, AP physics, AP English language, and honors computer science 3, but balanced her schedule with regular English and Spanish 5.

Francesca exuded responsibility and maturity. She had a calm, unflappable demeanor, but underneath, her wheels were always spinning. It was not surprising that the principal selected her as one of twenty students to lead a peer-training program to build awareness about the dangers of drugs and alcohol. She was the type of person who could connect with the nerdy computer science kids just as well as with the popular athletic kids. To her surprise, she was more comfortable with the nerdy computer science types, but given her social status in school and long-term relationships with the popular crowd, she initially felt embarrassed by this revelation.

Creating Francesca's College Application Wheel

I met Francesca during the spring of her junior year in high school. She impressed me on a number of levels. First, she was an incredibly striking, poised, and respectful young woman. As we went around the wheel, I circled intellectual curiosity and leadership as her two areas of strength. In looking at her rigorous schedule junior year, with seven hard academic subjects and a genuine interest in computer science, I knew right away that Francesca's interest in the STEM fields, and in particular her deep love of programming, was her angle. I asked her why she liked computer science so much. She told me in her humble yet confident manner, "It just comes easily to me. I like the logic behind it and I really love solving problems." She had attended an open house for girls in engineering at Columbia University and was impressed by the school and its offerings.

Francesca had already taken her SATs and did very well; she got a 740 in the math section, 720 in critical reading, and an 800 in writing. I suggested that she retake the SATs and aim for an 800 on the math section. (I would normally be doing somersaults if a student showed up with a 740 in math, but given how strong everything else was on Francesca's record and her desire to pursue computer science, I thought she should give it a go.) I also recommended that she take the math 2 and physics subject tests, aiming for an 800 in math 2 and 700+ in physics. She had taken the chemistry subject test as a sophomore.

Francesca ran track and cross-country at the varsity level. She was developing as a leader in her high school. She was selected by the principal to be part of the DREAM Team at her high school, a group of twenty students who educate their peers about the dangers of drugs and alcohol. She also was selected as a transition leader at her high school to help freshmen acclimate to high school and as a math and science tutor for the National Honor Society. Francesca had the desire to do even more because she realized that she was an effective leader. So we set out a plan for her to try to become captain of her cross-country team for her senior year.

Finally, we talked about her multicultural background and her travel experiences. She traveled often to Europe to visit her father's family. She also had traveled to England the previous summer with her honors English teacher and a group of students for two weeks. She enjoyed the experience of looking at a country from a literary point of view. She also participated in a Spanish exchange program with her high school and hosted a Spanish student for two weeks in her home. She continually looked for ways to get to know people from different cultures, which stemmed from her ability to move seamlessly among groups.

Francesca's Strengths

- Computer science/STEM girl
- Highly intelligent
- Understood herself and how best to achieve balance in her life
- Outstanding grades in a most challenging curriculum
- Leader in high school through DREAM Team, National Honor Society, transition leader, and cross-country
- Poised and confident

- Strong intellectual curiosity
- Multicultural family background and experiences
- Well liked by a wide range of students

Francesca's Weaknesses

- Limited community service
- Could improve math score on SAT for Ivies
- Had not done a lot of activities outside of high school community
- Had not extended intellectual curiosity outside of school classes through pre-college summer programs or other venues

Francesca's Checklist

Francesca had a stellar academic record. She pushed herself to highest level consistently in math and science and strategically in history, English, and foreign language. She was well liked by her teachers and peers. I advised her to take the SATs one more time to see if she could nudge her math score closer to 800. She also needed to take the math 2 and physics SAT subject tests and score in the mid to high 700s (possibly 800 in math 2).

Francesca was emerging as a leader in her high school in a number of ways: DREAM Team, transition leader, and National Honor Society. I told her she should try to become captain of the varsity cross-country team for her senior year. She felt fairly confident that she could achieve this. She also needed to continue programming and developing computer games on her own to show her intellectual curiosity and interest more deeply. She needed to also attend additional open houses aimed at girls in engineering or STEM fields at highly select colleges to demonstrate interest and see if she liked other schools as much as Columbia.

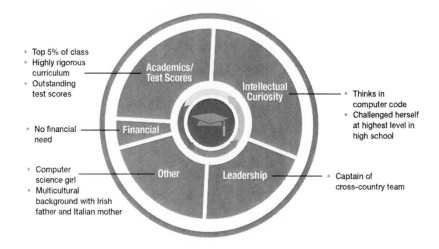

Francesca's Application Wheel: Fall of Senior Year

- **Academics:** Francesca had a stellar academic record. She had almost straight A's in the most rigorous curriculum available. She needed to continue pushing herself in math, English, science, and computer science, but could take academic levels in Spanish and history.

- **Test scores:** Francesca took the SATs one more time and reached her goal of 800 in math, 750 in critical reading, and 800 in writing (from her first sitting). She also got in the 700s for math 2 and physics, so she was in good shape for any Ivy League or highly selective university.

- **Athletics:** Francesca continued to focus on cross-country and track. She became captain of the cross-country team her senior year. Francesca did not want to pursue running at a Division I or Division III level, but would likely run at the club level when in college.

- **Special talent:** Francesca's ability to write code and create computer games for fun was her special talent.

- **Intellectual curiosity:** Francesca showed her intellectual curiosity through her challenging curriculum and her ability to manage a very heavy workload in a calm, determined manner. Taking three computer science courses on top of AP statistics, AP calculus BC, and AP physics also showed this. Her travel and cross-cultural exchange programs also demonstrated her intellectual curiosity.

- **Leadership:** Francesca emerged a leader in her high school community, taking on leadership roles in four separate areas within the school: DREAM Team, National Honor Society, transition leader, and captain of the cross-country team.
- **Other:** Francesca was a girl interested in computer science/STEM. Nationwide, less than 20 percent of computer science majors are girls, so this was definitely a big part of her angle.
- **Financial:** Francesca did not have financial need, but thought it would be nice to get merit aid if applicable.

Developing the College List

Francesca wanted a school with a strong pre-professional bent with excellent STEM majors and computer science. She wanted like-minded students who are interested in computer science and programming but also have other interests—"cool nerds." She wanted a diverse student body, but also wanted students with a similar background to hers. Francesca preferred a school with a core curriculum or clear learning objectives. She also wanted a prestigious school with access to her professors and a balance between work and play.

Key College Criteria for Francesca

- A medium to large university
- A distinct college campus near or in a city (Columbia and Penn were both a perfect combination of campus and city for her)
- Wanted to study computer science or something else in the STEM fields
- Brand name of the school was important
- Financial aid was not a deal breaker, but it would be nice to get some merit aid

- Would likely not join a sorority, but okay if there was Greek life on campus as long as it did not dominate the social scene
- Would like a more academic environment, but also wanted to have fun
- Would be nice to have the opportunity to run at the club level
- Internship and undergraduate research opportunities were important

The Final List

The Wild Cards

Normally called reaches, but Francesca was in the running for these schools, so they were more wild cards than reaches.

- **Columbia University:** Francesca attended a reception for girls interested in technology, and she felt very comfortable in the environment.
- **University of Pennsylvania:** Francesca fell in love with Penn after her visit. She loved the energy on campus and could see herself thriving there. She liked that she could take classes at the other colleges as well as in the School of Engineering. This was her top choice, and she wanted to apply early decision.

The Possibles

- **Carnegie Mellon University:** Their computer science program has an outstanding reputation. For any other major, Carnegie Mellon would be a likely school for Francesca; however, their computer science program is the most select program in the school.
- **Cornell University:** Francesca liked their program and the overall feel of the school. She was not crazy about its rural location.

The Likelies

- **Boston College:** This is a popular school for graduates from her high school, and Francesca liked the feel and location of the school.

- **Johns Hopkins University:** She felt comfortable with the student body, and it was close to home.
- **Tufts University:** Francesca really liked Tufts when she visited. She liked the quirky student body, the vibe on campus, and its proximity to Boston.

The Safeties

- **University of Maryland at College Park:** UMD is bigger than Francesca would have liked, but she would likely get into one of its honors programs and thought there would be a lot of good opportunities.
- **Stevens Institute of Technology:** She liked the campus and computer science opportunities when she visited. She would likely get merit money there as well.

Choosing an Essay Topic

Given Francesca's reserved nature, she and her parents wanted to make sure that all of her great strengths came through in her essays. I found that once we started brainstorming, it was clear that still waters do run deep. We identified several key themes.

- She enjoyed challenges and solving problems, both academically and socially.
- Family was a big part of her life. She had weekly Sunday dinners with her mom's large and loud extended Italian family, yet she took more after her dad's reserved English family. This familial contrast allowed Francesca to get along with and understand a wide range of people.
- She liked to be unique and march to her own beat.
- Up until physics and AP computer science, school had been highly formulaic for her and she had thrived. When she got into those classes, she was initially frustrated, but ended up loving them and the challenge, and learned how to solve those problems on her own just for fun.

Narrowing Down Possible Topics

Experience: Francesca's Major Experiences and Their Impacts

- **Taking AP computer science** (gave her confidence in own her nerdiness, but also taught her how to learn on her own). Francesca knew that taking AP computer science was both an academic and social risk, because not only was she one of the few girls in the class, she was also the only one of her friends in the class. She was initially embarrassed to tell her friends that she was taking it, for fear of being mocked. However, once she got into the class, she faced an even bigger fear: failure. On the first day of class, the teacher assumed that everyone had some programming background in Java (and most did). But Francesca had never programmed before and was initially too afraid to ask for help. Eventually, she did ask for help and was relieved that she was not the only one. She spent hours researching how to program and taught herself the basics until eventually she was the one others came to for help. She was happy that she took this risk because she felt like it set her apart from others and she discovered her passion.

- **Captain of the cross-country team** (evolved as a leader by thinking strategically about how to achieve her goal of becoming captain). When Francesca was a new freshman on the cross-country team, she looked up to the captains as they paraded around with confidence. She viewed the captains as the mascots for the team and the face of the team, and she wanted to become one of them from day one. Francesca realized that the key to becoming captain was getting the freshman team to like her. So, as a junior, she began cheering the freshman team and got to know them really well. She felt like their big sister, reminiscing about classes and teachers and finding a way to connect with them. She genuinely enjoyed their relationships, but she also knew strategically that the freshman team was the key to her becoming captain because they had the largest numbers. She became captain by a large margin and enjoyed a close relationship with her team.

- **Having an older diabetic cousin** (created a role reversal where Francesca became the mentor instead of the mentee). Her cousin developed diabetes when she was eleven years old. Up until then, Francesca had always looked up to her as the oldest cousin of a large brood, but her cousin did not manage the news well when she was diagnosed. Now the responsibility for taking care of all the younger cousins fell onto Francesca. At first she did not like her new role, but eventually she got used to it and even became a confidante to her older cousin. She also found that other family members confided in her because she was a good listener. Overall this experience made Francesca more grateful for the life she had and she enjoyed her new role as the family confidante.

Describe a Setback That You've Had and How You Learned from It

- **Getting C's at the beginning of physics** (taught her to dig in and work hard to understand something difficult). Francesca did not approach honors physics with the right mentality at the beginning of the year. Up until this class, everything came easily to her; she achieved straight A's with little outside studying. However, physics required visualizing everything rather than just learning a formula and applying it. After the first few tests, she realized that she was not taking this class seriously enough. She had to work really hard, take notes on problems, and stick with the homework until she finished all the problems, even if they were challenging. Eventually, Francesca came to love the challenge of figuring out the problems for herself, and physics became one of her favorite subjects, so much so that she took AP physics her senior year. She worked for it, but it was very satisfying in the end.

What Is the Most Quirky or Interesting Part of Your Background That Most People Don't Know about You?

- **She likes to write computer programs outside of school.** Francesca was writing a PC version of the popular computer game Bejeweled. She also wanted to create an app for iOS. She imagined an app that would register a runner's pace and correlate it with his or her music library. She figured that it won't be that hard since the music was already on the device, and the program would just need to loop through the songs to find the beat.

Person: Individuals Who Have Had a Significant Impact on Francesca's Life and Outlook

- **Dad** (taught her to love learning for learning's sake and do what she loves). Francesca's dad was incredibly smart, but he did not go to college; in fact, he dropped out of high school in England, where he grew up. Because of this, he instilled in Francesca a love of learning and the importance of education. He made up math quizzes for her when she was younger; they built a robot together when she was in fourth grade. He instilled in her a desire to find her passion and also be open to different points of view.

- **Maternal grandmother** (taught her to have a voice). Francesca's reserved nature came from her dad's side of the family. However, attending weekly Sunday dinners at her maternal grandma's house showed Francesca how to speak up with confidence. Her grandma's loud, opinionated voice ran through Francesca's mind every time she spoke her point in class or led her peers.

■ ■ ■ Possible Essay Topic Summary Chart ■ ■ ■

Experience and Its Impact

AP computer science
Developed her confidence in her ability to solve problems and embrace her inner nerd

Cross-country captain

Showed how thinking strategically can help her achieve her goals and become a strong leader

Role reversal with diabetic cousin

Forced her outside of her comfort zone, but allowed her to become a leader and confidante in her family

App development

Shows how her mind works with regard to computer science and its applications

Setback and Lessons Learned

C's in honors physics

Taught her how to work hard and found great satisfaction in learning for the sake of learning

Person and His or Her Impact

Father

Imparted values and a sense of humor

Director of *The Provoked Wife*

First adult who shared his sense of humor

Michael Moore

Source of political awakening

The Personal Statement Essay

Francesca wanted to write about her experience in AP computer science because it served as a pivotal point in her life as a student and as a person. She started by describing her initial reluctance to admit that she was taking this "geeky" class.

My first day of AP computer science was not what I expected or what I had hoped it would be. That morning, I was mocked by friends as they perused my schedule and came across the one class in the school reserved especially for "geeks and losers," two categories under which I never wished to fall.

She went on to describe how, in spite of her initial embarrassment, she actually felt most at home in this class.

> I trudged through the halls, avoiding eye contact with those who knew where I was headed, but upon entering the class, my mood was immediately lifted. This was the place where I felt most like myself—where I could express a sincere passion for learning without being ridiculed by friends. It did not matter that I was one of the only girls in my class, because I could program just as well as the boys.

However, her feeing of contentment was short lived because she came to realize that unlike in her Visual Basic class the previous year, where everyone started at the same level, in this class, many kids already knew how to program. For the first time in Francesca's life, she was not the top of the class.

> However, as my teacher wrote the instructions for our first project on the board, I stared blankly at words, which held no meaning for me. Never had it occurred to me to research Java tips over the summer. I looked around me to see everyone else already hard at work with their heads inches from their monitors and their fingers flying across the keyboards while I sat motionless without a clue where to begin.

So now Francesca had two hurdles to overcome.

> Not only was I taking a class that put my social status in jeopardy, but I couldn't even complete a beginner's project for that class.

She went on to describe her anger not only at her teacher for not giving specific directions (as her previous teachers always did), but mostly at herself for not being able to cope without them. But Francesca was not that easily discouraged. She went on to describe how she researched the problem on Google and tried to teach herself how to do the problem.

> I attempted to put together something resembling a program, but was confronted with errors that only multiplied themselves as the nights went on.

Francesca's story best addresses the Common Application prompt "Recount an incident or time when you experienced failure. How did it affect you, and what lessons did you learn?" She describes how her failure affected her initially, but, more important, she illustrates how she bounced back from her initial setback.

> I had been hesitant to ask for help because I was sure I would be laughed at for my lack of experience with Java. However, relief came immediately as I showed the boy sitting in front of me my error message and he responded, "Don't worry, I was having that same problem!" My confidence increased as I realized that I wasn't the only one having trouble and that my errors were mostly missing semicolons or brackets. I worked patiently with the rest of my classmates for the next week, and when the time came to hand in our projects, I was genuinely proud of my results.

She wrapped up the essay by showing what she learned from the experience and how it affected her.

> Because of the challenge I overcame, I found my first project in AP computer science more satisfying than any test I did well on in another class, no matter how frustrating it may have been to begin with. As the year progressed, I found that I was able to help my peers decipher their errors and discovered the satisfaction of collaboration. I excitedly shared with my friends all the different problems that could be accomplished with just a simple computer program, eventually convincing a friend to join me and the

army of nerds. I found that I no longer needed structure in the classroom, but instead craved independence and challenge.

This experience showed that Francesca grew not only as a student but also as a person. She no longer needed to hide her passion for computer science from her friends; instead she discovered how to share it with them. She also gained confidence in her ability to learn in an unstructured environment, which is critical for a highly select college.

The Short Answer

Francesca was asked to expand on one of her activities in more detail in the short answer. She wanted to focus on her leadership in cross-country for this piece and show how she became captain. We discussed how she could demonstrate her strategic approach without sounding calculating. She emphasized the way she built a community within the team by emulating the previous captains and leading by example.

> The first people I noticed when I joined the cross-country team were four girls parading around in high socks and neon bandannas, cheering on other training groups, and motivating teammates who were slacking. They were confident but not bossy, cheery but not annoying, and I desperately wanted to be one of them. Each year, I attempted to emulate the qualities which I knew set them apart as captains so that come senior year, I could lead the team to victory. I focused on the largest part of the team, the freshmen. I cheered until the last person crossed the finish line, I learned the names of every freshman, and I made sure they knew mine. I ended up becoming captain, not because I was the fastest or the most popular, but because I took the time to get to know my team. Because of the strong bonds I established with my team, I could relate to them more easily and lead them with confidence.

Supplemental Essays by School

Why This Academic Interest and This School?

Francesca knew that she wanted to major in computer science given her positive experience with AP computer science and the fact that computer code constantly circled through her mind. She told me how she imagined the computer code behind everything she saw, from a kitchen appliance to a glucose monitor. She had a strong desire to create programs that could impact the world and solve problems, and she wanted to acquire the skills to be the one leading the charge, so it was easy to make a case for "Why this academic interest?" Since Francesca was applying early decision to the University of Pennsylvania, she wanted to focus on its supplemental essay first and use that as a springboard for her other "Why this academic interest?" essays. She had several other supplements on hand in case she was deferred or denied early decision from Penn.

She started off this essay by bringing the reader into her mindset on how she thought in code.

I am on the fourth mile of a five-mile run when my iPod shuffles to "Scar Tissue" by the Red Hot Chili Peppers. The song is one of my favorites, but for the purpose of pacing it doesn't quite fit. I think to myself how much easier runs would be if I could find songs that match the pace I need and keep me going even when I feel like slowing down. Pieces of computer code start flying through my head, rapidly assembling themselves into a simple iOS app that accesses the user's desired pace and forms playlists to match the rhythm of their steps.

This helped us get into her mind, and from there she linked this passion to how she wanted to impact the world through computer science and, more specifically, how Penn would help her achieve her goals to address the "Why this school?" part of the prompt.

I am particularly interested in Penn's computer science department because it emphasizes teaching students how to apply what they learn to different aspects of life, rather than simply programming. Between courses such as "Introduction to Artificial Intelligence" and "Visualizing the Past," Penn merges engineering, liberal arts, and business with its computer science curriculum in a diverse way that appeals to me.

Anyone looking at Francesca's academic record could see that this was genuine. She consistently excelled across academic disciplines. She then tied her interest into non-academic pursuits to show how she would contribute to the campus.

I was also enthralled by how active and passionate every student was when I first made my way down Locust Walk. People everywhere were shouting out names of interesting clubs to join, and I felt compelled to stop and hear about the RoboCup and PennVention. As I listened to the students describing these competitions, I started imagining which of my programs might be strong enough to compete.

By putting herself on campus, she helped the admissions officers also visualize her as a student. She concluded by underscoring how she would contribute.

As a student passionate about engaging extracurriculars, rigorous coursework, and community service, I truly believe that I could fit seamlessly into the Penn matrix and leave my mark on the school and community.

Francesca used this structure for her other schools that required this essay, including Cornell, Johns Hopkins, and Carnegie Mellon. Tufts requires a "Why Tufts?" essay, so Francesca focused on the latter part of the essay and tailored it for Tufts. Columbia has a very short "Why this academic interest?" essay, which Francesca extracted and excerpted from the beginning of this essay. Finally, she used the first part of this essay for the University of Maryland prompt "What is your something?"

Let Your Life Speak/Describe Your Family Background

Francesca wrote a great essay describing her family dinners at her grandma's house. She talked about how her grandma's confidence resonated in her mind each time she spoke.

> I may lack the aggressive confidence that my grandma is known for, but my life still speaks from the head of the table. Every time I argue my opinion in history class or push my training group through a long run, I know that I am channeling a part of my Italian grandma into my voice. My grandma's unrelenting realism and penetrating voice guarantees that when my life speaks, it is always heard loud and clear.

She was able to use this essay to address the Tufts prompt "Let your life speak" and the University of Maryland write-your-own question, for which she wrote "Describe your family background."

Complementary Angles

Letters of Recommendation
- Francesca asked her AP computer science and honors physics teachers for letters of recommendation because they would be able to write about her strong work ethic and aptitude for STEM fields.
- She also got a letter of recommendation from her cross-country coach, who could speak to her leadership.

Brag Sheet/Resume
- Francesca's brag sheet emphasized her athletic accomplishments in track and cross-country, her strong leadership within her high

school, her cross-cultural travel experiences, and her aptitude and interest in science and computer science.

Supplemental Materials
- Francesca had no supplemental materials.

Additional Information
- Francesca did not have any extenuating circumstances to report in her record. She uploaded her detailed brag sheet/resume here.

Results

Francesca was accepted to Penn early decision. She also got accepted to the University of Maryland before she had a chance to withdraw her application.

Final Decision

University of Pennsylvania School of Engineering and Applied Science

What Can You Learn from Francesca's Story?
Questions to Ask Yourself

- Have you had any setbacks, academic or otherwise, in your life? How did they impact you? How did you recover? What did you learn from them?
- Do you have a passion that embarrasses you? Why? Do you pursue it anyway? How have you come to terms with it? Did you need to be embarrassed by it, or was it all in your head?
- What do you think about when you are not in school? In other words, what runs through your head when you are running, dancing, or performing community service? How can you channel that into something positive?
- Have you ever felt like you are not being true to yourself? Why? What is preventing you from admitting an interest? Fear? Embarrassment? How can you overcome this?

- What is your family background like? How have different sides of your family impacted you differently? What have you learned from them?
- What goals do you have? How can you develop a strategy to help you achieve your goals? Write down three things you can do to help yourself get there.

Notes

10

HUGH
THE SCIENTIST BY DAY,
THEATER AFICIONADO BY NIGHT

Lessons Learned during the Application Process

In this case, you will observe a sparring match between a Chinese father and his son. They shared a similar long-term goal of his becoming a physician; however, their ideas of the best path to achieve this goal differed. Hugh preferred to go the traditional route and attend a four-year liberal arts college first and then apply to medical school. His father wanted him to pursue an accelerated path that required getting accepted into a seven-year bachelor of arts/medical degree (BAMD) program as a freshman. This case will illustrate how to follow two paths simultaneously and how the process ultimately worked out to satisfy them both. Finally, this case will show you how important it is to follow your own passions while being mindful of your parents' wishes.

Hugh's Snapshot

- GPA: 5.43 (weighted, out of 6)
- Rigor: 21 AP/honors classes

- SAT: 1470/2260
- ACT with writing: N/A
- SAT subject tests: math 2: 800; biology: 780; chemistry: 730; US history: 790
- Class rank: top 10 percent

About Hugh

- Main interests: pre-med, music, theater/film
- Hugh was incredibly diligent and conscientious about his studies; he put a lot of pressure on himself and at times could become anxious about his performance.
- He had a sincere interest in science; however, he lit up when he talked about theater and pop culture. He discovered Manhattan during the beginning of his junior year and loved nothing more than tooling around New York City, seeing shows and sighting famous actors and celebrities.
- Hugh was also extremely talented musically and played the English horn and oboe in several ensembles; he also organized a group of his friends to play in senior homes.
- Hugh's parents were both raised in China and came to this country for graduate school. His mom was a physician and his dad had a PhD in science. They strongly believed in education as a means to success and instilled this philosophy of hard work and excellence in academics into Hugh.
- Finances would not determine where he went to school, but a seven-year accelerated medical school program would mean one less year to pay for.

Personality Profile

Hugh went to a highly competitive, predominantly Asian high school; he took the most rigorous curriculum available. His junior schedule resembled many students' senior schedules. with honors physics, AP statistics, AP language composition, AP calculus AB, AP US history, and Spanish honors 5. Yet despite being a highly motivated student with strong grades, at times he still felt inadequate among his über-high-achieving peers.

Hugh's parents' desire for him to become a doctor and his willingness to please them often clouded his true personality. Hugh was inquisitive, charismatic, highly musical, and sensitive. He adored the theater, sports, and all things pop culture, and at times obsessed over his passions. But he also had an interest in science and was struggling to find a way for both sides of his personality to coexist.

Creating Hugh's College Application Wheel

I met Hugh during the spring of his junior year in high school. His parents were interested in him pursuing an accelerated medical school program (BAMD) or alternatively attending a college with an excellent pre-med track. (Even though students do not major in pre-med, certain colleges have excellent pre-med advising and acceptance rates into medical schools.) At our first meeting, it became clear that Hugh's parents wanted him to go to an accelerated medical school program, but Hugh and I were not positive that this was the best approach. As I outlined the steps necessary to become competitive for this type of a program (summer research, 250+ hours of community service involving patient interaction, shadowing a doctor, 1500 SATs), Hugh looked overwhelmed. I tried to suggest that a seven-year medical school track is not always the best option for all students. His father agreed but insisted that we pursue the course and have a back-up plan in case it did not work out. Hugh's head hung down in tacit agreement.

So I continued with the meeting, attempting to support Hugh while satisfying his parents' desires. As previously mentioned, Hugh had an extremely rigorous schedule with mostly A's and B+'s in honors physics and honors Spanish 5. I suggested he try to go in for extra help and review the website Khanacademy.org to nudge his physics grade up to an A to put him in a good position for the seven-year BAMD programs. He had already taken the SATs twice when we met, receiving a score of 670 in critical reading, 760 in math, and 790 in writing. Unfortunately, most BAMD programs like to see a combined critical reading and math score of roughly 1400–1500. Hugh's scores put him in the running for some programs, but the more competitive programs required a 1490 minimum score for consideration. I recommended that he take them again with a goal of 1490+. Hugh had scored very well on three SAT subject tests in biology (780), math 2 (800), and chemistry (730). He wanted to take one more, so I suggested he take the US history subject test right after he took the AP exam to minimize his studying.

Hugh played the oboe and English horn at a high level. He was first chair both in the regional band and in all-state band. We set a goal for him to audition for the all-Eastern band as well as record a track for his arts supplement. Hugh also organized several of his friends to play weekly in a nursing home. He was going to continue this because he enjoyed the interactions with the senior residents and it could count toward his community service hours for the seven-year medical programs.

We also talked about ways that Hugh could make himself more competitive for the seven-year BAMD programs. He had interned in a lab the prior summer. I asked him to describe his experience to me. He started, "Well, I don't really remember exactly what I did, but I filed samples and looked at tissues under the microscope. I mostly just observed what was going on in the lab."

I probed, "Do you remember what you learned or what you liked about the experience? Did you keep a journal about the experience?"

His father interjected, "Hugh, see this is why you have to pay attention! You need to keep notes!" Dejected, Hugh tried to remember, but it was clear to me that his heart was not in it.

I decided to take a different tack. "Hugh, tell me a little bit about what else you like to do for fun," I asked.

"Well, I love going into Manhattan and exploring the city and seeing shows. I saw *How to Succeed in Business without Really Trying* with Daniel Radcliffe. It was amazing. Have you seen it?" he gushed.

"Yes, I did see it and it was amazing," I replied. "I was so impressed with how good Daniel Radcliffe was in the role. It was unexpected."

We continued in this vein, exchanging our interest and love of the theater. Finally I saw the true Hugh. He was excited, passionate, and certain in his convictions. I commented to his parents how much more animated Hugh was in talking about theater and that perhaps he should consider alternative routes to medical school. They agreed to pursue a dual path, but not to abandon their dream of Hugh aiming for an accelerated medical school program. So we finished the meeting with an agreement to position Hugh to compete in a seven-year BAMD program while being open to other options if one of these programs did not work out.

Hugh's Strengths

- Intellectually curious about science, pop culture, and theater
- Extremely diligent student, at times obsessive
- Talented musician in sought-after instruments (oboe and English horn)
- Excellent grades in a most challenging curriculum
- Clear angle with science and music
- Strong work ethic
- Lab experience
- Some community service
- Starting to find his own voice and broaden his parents' definition of success

Hugh's Weaknesses

- SATs on low side for BAMD programs (particularly in critical reading)
- Would need more hours of community service for BAMD programs
- Not 100 percent committed to BAMD program and receiving strong pressure from parents
- Self-confidence could be improved; put a lot of pressure on himself

Hugh's Checklist

Hugh had a strong academic record with a highly rigorous curriculum and good grades. Given his desire to pursue a seven-year BAMD program, he needed to try to improve his grade in honors physics from a B+ to an A by going in for extra help and watching online tutorials. He needed to take the SATs one more time to see if he could improve his critical reading score to a 700 to put him in the running for the more competitive programs.

Hugh was a talented musician and needed to continue to participate in music at the highest level. I advised that he should also prepare a CD showcasing his musical talent for the arts supplement. As he wanted to pursue a BAMD program, he needed to increase his hours in community service and in particular find community service that involved patient interaction. His volunteer hours playing music at the nursing home would count toward this. He also needed to try to volunteer at a hospital over the summer as well as get more experience doing research in a lab. I recommended that he attend a pre-college summer program related to medicine to give him more exposure to the various types of medicine he could pursue. Finally, he needed to arrange to shadow a couple of physicians so that he had a better understanding of what the day-to-day life of a physician entails.

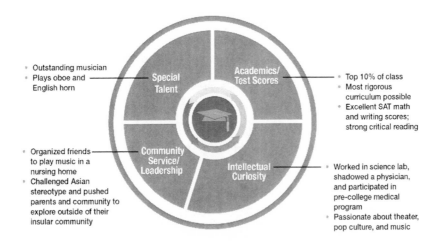

Hugh's Application Wheel: Fall of Senior Year

- **Academics:** Hugh had a strong academic record with mostly A's and a few B+'s sprinkled in. He needed to continue with his academically rigorous curriculum in his senior year.
- **Test scores:** Hugh took the SATs two more times after our initial meeting, and though he did not reach his goal of 700 in the critical reading section, he did improve his scores to 690 in critical reading and 780 in math for a combined score of 1470. He was in the running for many of the BAMD programs, but not the most competitive ones.
- **Athletics:** This was not a part of Hugh's wheel.
- **Special talent:** Hugh was a talented musician, playing the oboe and the English horn. He created a recording of his playing to submit as part of the arts supplement to schools that accept one.
- **Intellectual curiosity:** Hugh showed his intellectual curiosity in science and cell death and growth through his two stints working in a lab, his rigorous high school curriculum, and his participation in a Georgetown University Medical Institute pre-college program. His interest in pop culture and theater also demonstrated his intellectual curiosity.
- **Leadership:** Hugh organized a group of musicians to play in a nursing home for senior residents for more than two years. He was also first chair English horn and oboe in a regional band. He also initiated outings into New York among his friends and family.
- **Other:** Hugh's parents were both raised in China, so he was a first-generation American. He showed strength of character by rebelling against their rigid, academically focused upbringing and trying to introduce his family and friends to theater, sports, and other non-academic pastimes.
- **Financial:** Hugh's decision would not be driven by finances, but the seven-year accelerated medical school program was more attractive because it would shave off one year of tuition.

Developing the College List

Hugh and his parents wanted to focus on accelerated medical programs or liberal arts colleges with strong science and pre-med opportunities. Hugh liked to be engaged in class discussions and preferred a smaller college with a flexible curriculum and easy access to his professors (unless it was an accelerated medical program). He preferred a more hipster, artsy, cosmopolitan student body with a liberal political view. Overall, he preferred a more intellectual environment, but also wanted to have fun.

Key College Criteria for Hugh

- Small to medium school, or an honors college within a larger university
- A residential, distinct campus, preferably near a big city or at least an active cultural city
- Wanted to study abroad
- Preferred a secular environment, but wanted some Asian population
- Nice if there was some sports presence and school spirit
- Opportunity to participate in intramural sports, music, and community service
- Brand name of the school was important to him (unless it is an accelerated medical program)
- Internship and undergraduate research opportunities were important
- Financial aid would not impact his decision, but it would be nice to get some merit aid

The Final List

Since Hugh had dueling desires—a small liberal arts experience versus an accelerated medical program—we essentially developed two lists of schools. Hugh ended up applying to twenty-two schools—a record for one of my clients!

The Reaches: Accelerated Medical Programs

- **Boston University:** Hugh liked the location and it has an excellent accelerated medical program.
- **Drew University/New Jersey Medical School:** This program was in Hugh's home state, so he had a slightly higher chance of acceptance.
- **Drexel University:** Accelerated medical program.
- **George Washington University:** Hugh liked the location and it has an excellent program.
- **University of Miami:** This school has an accelerated medical program.
- **The College of New Jersey/New Jersey Medical School:** This was Hugh's first choice among the accelerated programs; however, it was unlikely since they had a minimum critical reading/math SAT score of 1490 and Hugh was just shy of that number.
- **Pennsylvania State University:** Penn State has an accelerated medical program.
- **University of Rochester:** This school has an accelerated medical program, an excellent music school, and open curriculum.

The Reaches: Four-Year Colleges

- **Amherst College:** Hugh loved the diverse, intellectual environment and open curriculum. He thought it was a long shot, but he wanted to apply because he felt so comfortable on campus.
- **Brown University:** Hugh loved the open curriculum and diverse student body. He considered applying to their combined eight-year medical school program, but decided to just apply to the college.
- **Harvard University:** Hugh knew this was a far reach, but figured what the heck? It's Harvard.
- **University of Pennsylvania:** Penn was another reach, but Hugh liked the energy and the urban campus, so wanted to try.

The Possibles: Accelerated Medical Programs

- **Rensselaer Polytechnic Institute/Albany Medical College:** RPI has an accelerated medical program.
- **Union College/Albany Medical College:** Hugh liked the liberal arts college aspect and it has an accelerated medical program.
- **Virginia Commonwealth University:** This school has an accelerated medical program.

The Possibles: Four-Year Colleges

- **Boston College:** Hugh liked the location and the "rah-rah" aspect of the school. He did not mind that it is a Jesuit school because it has strong pre-med and science programs.
- **Swarthmore College:** Hugh liked the intellectual community and access to Philadelphia. He could see himself going to college here.
- **Vanderbilt:** Hugh liked the strong school spirit and what he read. I worried that it might be too Greek for him.

The Likelies

- **Brandeis University:** It has excellent science and pre-med programs. Hugh felt comfortable on campus and liked the small liberal arts feel within a larger research institution. He also liked the proximity to Boston.
- **University of Michigan:** Hugh's parents had done some postgraduate work at the University of Michigan, so there was a familiarity with the school. It also has a good honors program.
- **New York University:** Even though there was no distinct campus, Hugh loved New York City and would have been happy to go to school here.

The Safety

- **Rutgers:** Strong science program, and tuition was right price.

Choosing an Essay Topic

Hugh identified several themes within his life (and surprisingly few of them had to do with medicine).

- He learned over time that it is more important to find people with like-minded interests than prejudging people.
- Life does not always work out the way you want it to, and he had to learn to let go somewhat and make the best of things.
- After a recent visit to China with his parents and seeing the poor conditions in the Chinese countryside, he developed a new understanding of why his parents push education so much.
- He had a desire to help others after seeing his grandfather dying of cancer and realizing that he could do nothing to stop his demise. This spawned his desire to go into medicine.

Narrowing Down Possible Topics

Experience: Hugh's Major Experiences and Their Impacts

- **Attending an Australian film festival and meeting actor Hugh Jackman** (made him realize that he could do anything if he worked hard at it). Hugh attended an Australian film festival where he got to meet his idol and namesake, Hugh Jackman. In Hugh's words, "Before intermission I went to the side of the stage and then I followed him to the bathroom. I essentially mobbed him to get his autograph. Even though he was a little annoyed, I felt empowered. It made me realize that if I want something, I will do whatever it takes to get it." Hugh always loved Jackman's movies, and then he researched more about Jackman's background and discovered that he was on Broadway. He liked that he was equally comfortable in Hollywood and on Broadway. The movie in the film festival was called *Real Steel* and featured a futuristic society. Jackman and his son in the movie showed how underdogs should never give up. Hugh related to this because he often felt like the underdog in his highly competitive high school. After seeing this movie he tried to be more outgoing and work harder.

- **Music** (the one place where all his worries went away). When Hugh plays music in an orchestra or band, all of his worries disappear. He especially liked the all-state band because the musicians there loved music as much as he did and he felt united with them.

- **Running** (made him happy). Hugh initially started running to get in shape, but then he realized how much it helped him mentally. He always felt happier and more relaxed after he ran.

- **His visit to China** (gave him a better understanding of his parents and prompted him to volunteer in a nursing home). He visited the countryside and saw bathrooms where he had to squat; he never realized how bad the conditions were where his parents grew up. The trip gave him a much greater appreciation for his parents. His parents are obsessed solely with academics, but after that trip he understood more why that was so. Nonetheless, he felt more American than Chinese and he resented their Chinese single-minded focus on homework. He pushed them to broaden their perspective, and they gradually became more lenient with him. That trip also allowed him to spend time with his grandfather, who was dying from cancer. Hugh felt powerless to help him, so when he came back to the United States he decided to volunteer in a nursing home. He organized some of his friends to play music, and he felt good about seeing the joy that his music brought to the seniors in the home. In a small way he felt like he was making a difference.

Describe a Setback That You've Had and How You Learned from It

- **Being treated unfairly by his band teacher** (taught him to accept decisions gracefully and move on). In spite of making all-state band during his freshman year, Hugh did not make his school's wind ensemble (the highest-level band) because there was no room for another English horn or oboe. Hugh was angry about this decision and felt that he was being treated unfairly. As a freshman, he was concerned that somehow he had been subjugated to a lower status and that he would look bad among his peers. He tried to fight it and asked for a higher ranking, but to no avail. He brooded for that year, refusing to practice until he participated in all-state band. Once he started enjoying music again for the sake of music and not status, he realized that he had been immature and finally accepted it and moved on.

Person: Individuals Who Have Had a Significant Impact on Hugh's Life and Outlook

- **All-state band conductor** (restored his love of music). The all-state band conductor exuded passion and joy regarding music. He told the students a story about how when he was in college, one of his professors asked the students to raise their hand if there was anything else besides music that they considered doing. This conductor was the only one whose hand stayed down. He motivated Hugh to strive to find something that he is truly passionate about and also reminded Hugh why he began playing music in the first place, not for status, but for personal and communal joy.

- **Holden Caulfield from *The Catcher in the Rye*** (Hugh found a like-minded individual). Hugh related to how Holden found everyone a phony. Hugh used to try to be friends with the popular kids, but ultimately found their relationships fake and limiting. Hugh no longer strived to be popular; instead he hung out with people who shared similar interests with him in film, music, and sports. He liked to hang out with kids from different groups and no longer classified people by group but just took them for who they were. As a result, Hugh was much happier.

What Is the Most Quirky or Interesting Part of Your Background That Most People Don't Know about You?

- **Hugh would like to be a spy.** He liked the sense of adventure.

■ ■ ■ Possible Essay Topic Summary Chart ■ ■ ■

Experience and Its Impact

Meeting Hugh Jackman

Empowered him to move toward his dreams and fight his underdog status

Music

Helped him find his true passion and find an environment where he can just be and not worry

Running

Found an healthy outlet to relax and stay fit

Visit to China

Gave him insight into his parents' background, and seeing his grandfather dying of cancer inspired him to volunteer in a nursing home

Setback and Lessons Learned

Not making wind ensemble freshman year

Taught him to accept setbacks and not be so worried about status, but instead focus on music for pleasure and sense of unity

Person and His or Her Impact

All state conductor

Modeled the importance of following one's true passion; restored love of music

Holden Caulfield

Helped him realize that he should worry less about popularity and more about finding genuine friends

The Personal Statement Essay

Hugh chose to write his main personal statement for the Common Application about his negative reaction to not making wind ensemble his sophomore year of high school and how he ultimately came around after participating in the all-state symphonic band. When he left my office, I had doubts about how strong an essay he could produce on this topic given the level of schools that he wanted to attend. My doubts quickly disappeared when I read his first draft and tears welled in my eyes from his heartfelt emotion on this topic.

> From the time in fourth grade when my flimsy, fragile hands picked up a makeshift plastic oboe in wonderment until my freshman year in high school when I proudly wielded an F.Lorée apparatus finely handcrafted in Paris from carefully selected pieces of granadilla wood, I rejoiced at the prospect of making music daily. The initial incentive was to try something unique and unorthodox; the oboe's lush, ethereal voice was my ideal candidate.

He then described how his feelings changed when he did not make wind ensemble, which to him seemed unfair and a slap in the face based on his perceived talent.

> That is, however, until sophomore year, when I did not secure a spot in my school's wind ensemble, a surreal yet devastating experience. I refused to come to terms with this setback. I experienced dual emotions of indignation and melancholy that pervaded my actions and thoughts 24/7. I no longer cared; rather, I felt that my pouting and brooding were justified. I stopped practicing cold turkey for a several months and exhibited subtle acts of irresponsibility and neglect to avenge my sufferings. This only exacerbated my teacher's distaste of me.

He recognized that he did not handle this failure with grace and maturity. And then he showed us how he changed his point of view because of an outstanding conductor.

I probably would have committed musical suicide and wasted six prior years of hard work had I not met my sophomore year conductor for state symphonic band. Though he was not a man of great stature, the music savant was a man of charisma and passion, filling the whole practice room with musical revelry through osmosis.

I listened avidly as he imparted us with his numerous musical experiences. Hours felt like mere minutes, and by the end of the day, we would groan in disappointment. Each day my love for music was restored bit by bit. On the day of the concert, he said, "Music is unique; during the moments an ensemble plays together all barriers—racial, political, social, and personal disagreements— disappear; that's the beauty virtually nothing else can achieve."

Hugh continued to illustrate how he came full circle back to music and realized the error of his ways. Hugh's story best addresses the Common Application prompt "Recount an incident or time when you experienced failure. How did it affect you, and what lessons did you learn?" He talked about his initial reaction to failure as immature, but ultimately realized the music was much more important to him and life than what level of band he was in.

At once, I looked back on my life and thought of how this maxim made complete sense. As I pieced my shattered puzzle set back together, I knew subconsciously that this was the real reason I played the oboe.

However, it could also speak to the prompt "Describe a place or environment where you are perfectly content. What do you do or experience there, and why is it meaningful to you?" because he went on to describe why this environment was so meaningful to him.

> During the moments we played together as an ensemble, I was at complete peace. All of my troubles disappeared. Before parting, I went up and thanked him sincerely, shedding tears of appreciation and disappointment in having to leave.

It could even work for the Common Application prompt "Discuss an accomplishment or event, formal or informal, that marked your transition from childhood to adulthood within your culture, community, or family." For this prompt, one could argue that his reaction to not making his high school's wind ensemble was one of a petulant child, but his experience participating in the all-state symphony band helped him transition into an adult because he looked beyond his own needs and recognized the experience as a whole. He concluded his essay writing:

> Now that I had something to strive for, I left inspired to work as hard as I could to continue to perfect my tone and playing ability. Through music, I could help promote harmony in any dispute or conflict. And though I cannot affect revolutionary changes on a mass scale, I can impact my community. Whether it is playing for rambunctious school children or volatile teens, I no longer care about the prestige. Instead, I look to music to learn more about myself, my instrument, and those around me.

This experience demonstrated that Hugh grew not only as a musician but also as a person. He did not need the status of group to validate his pleasure; he just needed to find a way to unite with others and share his passion. He developed insight into his past behavior and recognized his past immaturity. This story showed Hugh's resilience and self-awareness, which demonstrated his readiness to succeed in college.

The Short Answer

Hugh was asked to expand on one of his activities in more detail in the short answer. He wanted to talk about how his visit to his dying grandfather in China spawned his desire to volunteer in a nursing home by organizing a group of friends to play music. While he wrote his main essay about his passion for music, this short essay focused on how he used his music to make a difference and also laid the foundation for his interest in medicine.

At age thirteen, I watched helplessly as cancer consumed my grandfather's soul. I desperately wanted to help, but since I couldn't cure his cancer, I didn't know how. Upon returning from China, I volunteered at a senior home, hoping to be of use. On my first day, I recoiled in anxiety as a gaunt man grasped my oboe while I played. The nurse reassured me so I continued. I learned that the man, Steve, had dementia. As I performed more regularly, I started to enjoy our frequent interactions. Slowly, I developed empathy understanding his daily struggle to talk and move. On some days, Steve was absent-minded, but on others, I could see that sparkle in his eyes as if my music served as a temporary elixir and gateway to his previous warmhearted days. Alas, I found a way to aid the elderly by providing them psychological relief in their late stage lives. Thanks to him, I redefined my concept of assisting others realizing that I do not need to be the next Einstein in order to make a difference.

Supplemental Essays by School

Since Hugh was applying to so many schools, the supplemental essays could have been insurmountable. Yet Hugh powered through them systematically and with great flair. Thankfully, he was able to tweak one of his essays to fit the majority of his supplemental essays for his non–accelerated medical school programs. He also had to write a "Why medicine and why an accelerated program?" essay for all of his accelerated medical school programs along with numerous follow-up short answers at each juncture. His essays fell into the following categories.

Why This Academic Interest and This School?
Hugh knew he was going to follow a pre-med, scientific track coupled with music. He brought in his summer experience to show that he had two different sides of his personality that he hoped to pursue in college. He started off each of his essays explaining his dual interests.

> This past summer I spent three weeks shadowing a pathologist at Beth Israel Deaconess Medical Center in New York. By day, I was immersed in grand rounds, where pathologists discussed interesting cases among each other. I was fascinated by how they collaboratively diagnosed particularly challenging cases. Furthermore, I was captivated when viewing the cancerous aberrations caused by enlarged nuclei of the neurons, epithelial, intestinal, or whatever cells pathologists happen to be studying. By night, my aesthetic side kicked as I explored the theater, music, and film district of Midtown. By attending Broadway plays, talk shows, and films, I expanded my cosmopolitan outlook of the world.

This set the scene for where his academic interests lie. Then he connected this with how he would pursue these interests to answer the "Why this school?" part of the prompt. He started off with his academic pursuits and tied them to his background and passion for science.

> The College of Literature, Science, and the Arts at the University of Michigan is best suited for me because its liberal arts curriculum will allow me to explore my many interests. Last summer, I engaged in neurodegenerative disease research at Weill Cornell Medical Center. I found it particularly fascinating how a single anomaly in the brain, the backbone of bodily operations, could disrupt a person's health so drastically. At Michigan I hope to major in neuroscience. Additionally, I could take a wide range of classes from cellular and molecular biology to ecology and evolutionary biology to explore these and other phenomena

further. I also hope to further pursue these interests by doing research [in a particular lab].

And then he brought in his musical side and how he could grow his talent at Michigan.

Meanwhile, to cultivate my aesthetic sense, I would like to stay involved in music at the University of Michigan School of Music, Theatre, and Dance by continuing to study oboe. To take my skills further and improve my collaborative playing abilities, I hope to participate in the Campus Symphony or Philharmonia Orchestra of the strings department for non-music majors. And, if qualified, I would like to participate in the orchestral production aspect of a musical theater, as I am an avid Broadway aficionado. Having observed University of Michigan's theater alumni David Alan Grier and James Earl Jones in the productions of *Porgy and Bess* and *The Best Man* respectively, I look forward to seeing the rising talent that Michigan will train.

By putting himself on campus in a specific way, he helped the admissions officers to visualize him as a student.

Hugh used this structure for the University of Pennsylvania, which has a similar essay. He focused on the academic interests part of the essay for the schools that ask "Why this academic interest?" including Brown and NYU. For the "Why this school?" essays at Brandeis and Swarthmore, he kept the general theme, but focused more on second part of the essay.

Describe Your Family Background/Describe One of Your Communities and Your Role/Optional Topic Essay

Hugh wrote an honest essay about the pressure of growing up in a stereotypical first-generation Asian household and how he broke away from his parents' expectations after a serendipitous trip to New York City. He called this his "Asian stereotype" essay. The essay turned out to be extremely flexible in answering a wide range of prompts as it addressed his family background, his sense of community, his challenging of a particular ideal, and his role as a leader in changing his parents' and community's ideal.

"Hugh, if you get a B+, you will be grounded."

Before middle school, I lived a carefree existence, but by sixth grade, this became my parents' new mantra. They continually pressured me and I slowly began the path of becoming a stereotypical Asian American: intelligent, reserved, and awkward. At first I enjoyed my academic success, but soon the Asian mentality was too much to bear. Failing to maintain minimal standards, I began to slip.

Hugh continues to describe how his outlook changed for the better.

My dismal outlook would have continued if not for a serendipitous trip to New York for schoolwork. Upon setting foot in Times Square, I opened my eyes in amazement, viewing New York for the first time unfiltered by my parents. I was lost in the joy at the sight of its diversity of people, communities, and views. Everybody's niche existed in this liberal, metropolitan melting pot.

Next he explained how this trip opened up not only a new world, but also a new mindset of how he wanted to live his life.

Inspired by the city's variety and open-mindedness, I thought about what I truly loved: movies, music, theater, and sports. Proceeding with a cleansed and invigorated mind, I toured Manhattan's Broadway district, listened to street singers rallying up the Christmas fervor, and obtained school credit for visiting sites like the Metropolitan Museum of Art. New York was my savior, freeing the chains that lay obdurately intact on my shoulder for years.

Finally he concluded with how he grew.

> Returning home that day, I began paving a new path. While maintaining my hard-work ethic, I pursued my passions endlessly by going to Knicks games, attending Broadway shows and film festivals, and perfecting my oboe technique. While I have not given up that Asian identity completely, I have created a more fulfilling concoction, resulting in happiness and, more important, my individualism.

For the schools that asked about his role in the community (University of Michigan) or whether he is immovable, moves, or is a mover (University of Pennsylvania), he altered the ending to reflect how he changed not only himself but also others.

> Returning home that day, I began paving a new path. While maintaining my Asian attributes, I "Americanized" my parents and community, exposing them to various societies; I dragged them to Knicks game, Broadway shows, and film festivals. Serving as a gateway, I became a catalyst, inciting others in my community to lead a more balanced, varied life.

Hugh wrote seven different variations of this essay, adjusting the endings or adding different wording to address the specific prompts.

Why an Accelerated Medical Program?

Hugh had to write a variation of this essay for all of his accelerated medical school programs. Similar to what he did with his "Why this academic interest?" and "Why this school?" essays, he tailored the second part of the essay to focus on the specific attributes of each school in terms of curriculum, research opportunities, and extracurricular options. He also addressed the cost factor and the reduced pressure of knowing that he would be already accepted to medical school as his reasons for why he wanted to attend an accelerated program.

Complementary Angles

Letters of Recommendation
- Hugh asked his English and chemistry teachers to write letters of recommendation to show his different sides.
- He also got a letter from his mentor in the lab where he worked over the summer for the accelerated medical programs.

Brag Sheet/Resume
- Hugh emphasized his musical, science, and community service activities on his detailed brag sheet.

Supplemental Materials
- Hugh submitted an arts supplement of a recording of him playing the oboe for all schools that accepted one.

Additional Information
- Hugh did not have any extenuating circumstances to report in his record. This is, however, where he uploaded his detailed brag sheet/resume.

Interviews
- Hugh received interviews for Union and RPI's seven-year medical school programs. He was extremely nervous for the interviews, so we conducted several mock interviews to help assuage his nerves.

Results

Hugh had great results among his non–accelerated medical programs, which was not surprising given that his heart was never truly in the accelerated programs. He did, however, push through the process and go on a couple of interviews for the accelerated programs. He got accepted early action (nonbinding) to the University of Michigan Honors College, Boston College, and Rutgers. By the end of December, it became clear that he had not received interviews for most of the accelerated programs, and we discussed changing his application to early decision 2 (a January deadline) for Swarthmore, a school at which he really saw himself thriving. Since the Union and RPI accelerated programs were still in the running, his father wanted him to play it out since he already had two excellent options with Boston College and University of Michigan. Hugh became immune to other acceptances because in his mind, he knew he would not be accepted to any of the Ivies or Amherst, but he felt like he had a chance at Swarthmore, and, in his heart of hearts, he wanted that sort of academic experience. So we waited, hoping that it would work out in his favor.

And then, something miraculous happened: He got an acceptance letter about a week or two earlier than typical from Amherst and was waitlisted at Union and RPI's accelerated medical school programs. Hugh was practically in tears when he got the letter from Amherst. He asked me if it was real since he was given early notification as part of their diversity initiative. "Yes! This is real, Hugh. You did it, I am thrilled for you!"

He replied, "Part of me really hopes that I don't get into the seven-year program because I really want to go to Amherst!"

Thankfully, Hugh did not get off the waitlist, and when the denials came from his other reach schools, including Swarthmore, he no longer cared. Before he sent his deposit to Amherst, he asked me if I was sure that he could still get into a good medical school coming from Amherst. I sent him the medical acceptance rates from Amherst, which are well over 90 percent. He smiled and said, "I guess I don't need to worry!"

The Reaches: Accelerated Medical Programs

- **Boston University:** Denied
- **Drew University/New Jersey Medical School:** Denied
- **Drexel University:** Denied
- **George Washington University:** Denied
- **University of Miami:** Denied
- **The College of New Jersey/New Jersey Medical School:** Denied

- **Pennsylvania State University:** Denied
- **University of Rochester:** Accepted to University of Rochester; denied accelerated medical program

The Reaches: Four-Year Colleges
- **Amherst College:** Accepted
- **Brown University:** Denied
- **Harvard University:** Denied
- **University of Pennsylvania:** Denied

The Possibles: Accelerated Medical Programs
- **Rensselaer Polytechnic Institute/Albany Medical School:** Invited to interview; waitlisted
- **Union College/Albany Medical College:** Invited to interview; waitlisted
- **Virginia Commonwealth University:** Made it to second round; denied

The Possibles: Four-Year Colleges
- **Boston College:** Accepted
- **Swarthmore College:** Denied
- **Vanderbilt:** Waitlisted; withdrew

The Likelies
- **Brandeis University:** Accepted
- **University of Michigan:** Accepted into its honors program
- **New York University:** Accepted

The Safety
- **Rutgers:** Accepted into its honors program

Final Decision
Amherst College

What Can You Learn from Hugh's Story?
Questions to Ask Yourself

- Have you reacted badly to a disappointment? How and when did you realize your mistake? How did you right yourself? What did you learn?

- Do you and your parents have different ideas about the right path for you to take? How can you bring your parents to your point of view while still making them feel part of the process? (For parents: Are you imposing your own views on your child? If so, is this the right path? Can you try to see your child's perspective and find a way to satisfy both of your needs?)

- How has your family life impacted your life philosophy? How have you been able to incorporate these ideals and move beyond them?

- What are your true passions? How do they manifest themselves in your actions?

- What do you want out of college? How does this differ from what your parents want? How can you help them see your perspective?

- What is getting in the way of your happiness? How can you make a positive change in your attitude to help you find happiness? Write down three things you can do.

Notes

11

VEEMA
THE FIRST-GENERATION
CREATIVE WRITER
AND SOCIAL ACTIVIST

Lessons Learned during the Application Process

In this case, you will see how Veema found her angle by using her special talent in writing as a vehicle to overcome adversity and ADHD. She had below-average grades with an above-average curriculum and test scores, but she did not let her challenges stand in her way. In fact, she used them a source for inspiration in her writing and advocacy work. You will also learn how to explain bumps along the way in a matter-of-fact yet positive way.

Veema's Snapshot

- GPA: 3.0 GPA (weighted, out of 4.5)
- Rigor: 3 AP/honors classes
- SAT: 1220/1910
- ACT with writing: 27
- Class rank: bottom 50 percent

About Veema

- Main interests: creative writing, photography, and French
- Veema underwent numerous personal challenges during her freshman and sophomore years, which impacted her performance, but as her life became more stable in her junior year, her grade history reflected these changes.
- She was very sensitive and creative; she channeled her creativity into poems, short stories, and photography.
- She had ADHD, but she learned how to manage it.
- Veema's parents divorced when she was very young, and her father lived in India. She grew up with her mom and her grandmother in an overprotective maternal household. During Veema's first two years of high school, her grandmother passed away, her mom remarried and had a baby, and the family moved to a different school district.
- Finances would factor into where Veema went to school because with the addition of her stepfather's income, she would not qualify for financial aid; therefore, merit aid would be critical if she wanted to go to a small private liberal arts college.

Personality Profile

Veema went through a lot of changes during the early part of high school. During middle school and the early part of high school, she was shy and reserved, not 100 percent comfortable in her skin. However, when we met, her leadership qualities were starting to emerge. She took a lot of satisfaction from organizing events for the Red Cross club at her school. She also enjoyed French and writing poems and somewhat macabre short stories.

Veema's mother had recently remarried and had a baby in the course of two years. They moved from a smaller apartment to a house in a very competitive school district at the beginning of her high school years. As a result of all of the changes, Veema had to become much more independent, which at first was challenging but ultimately proved beneficial to her personal growth and self-confidence.

Creating Veema's College Application Wheel

I met Veema and her family during the spring of her junior year in high school. She arrived with her mother, stepfather, and baby brother in tow. Her stepfather had put together a spreadsheet showing the progression of Veema's grades through the middle of junior year. Her trajectory went from a mix of C+'s, B+'s, and one A– freshman year, to mostly Cs, one B–, and one A sophomore year, to mostly B+'s and A–'s junior year. She also got A's in all of her art-related electives and a B+ in her creative writing and film classes. I liked that her grades were on an upward swing, so I asked Veema to explain to me what was different about junior year. She said, "Well, when I started high school, my mom thought I was doing okay and that I didn't need to take my ADHD medication anymore so I stopped taking it. And you can see what happened."

"So did you start taking it again junior year? Was that the only change?" I asked.

"Yes, I did start taking it again, and I also just got more used to the new high school. I changed schools in the middle of ninth grade and it was much harder and bigger than my old school. It took me a while to get used to the changes."

We set out a plan for her to maintain her good grades and see if she could do equally well on her SATs or ACTs with writing. We set a goal of 600+ in each section of the SATs and 27+ for the ACTs with writing. The upswing in grades coupled with solid test scores would put her in a good position for applying to college as long as she could maintain good grades through the first marking period of senior year and could explain her situation.

As we worked our way around the wheel, it became clear that Veema had several special talents in creative writing and art. Veema had one of her short stories published in her school's literary magazine, and she had excelled in all of her art classes. We discussed taking some photography classes outside of school to see if this was an area that she really wanted to pursue. She was also going to apply for a summer internship through her high school to work with a photographer, and if that didn't work out, she thought about finding a job or doing some volunteer work in India.

Veema also emerged as a leader and was hoping to become president of her high school's Red Cross club. She was also very active in the Gay-Straight Alliance at her high school and the Help Darfur Now Club. As she became more independent, she found her voice both through her writing and through her activism. She no longer depended on her mom and grandmother for her opinions.

Veema's Strengths

- Creative, good writer, and improved grades
- Emerging leader and improved self-confidence
- Found her voice and passionate about supporting causes such as the Red Cross club, LBGTQ rights, and Help Darfur Now Club
- Overcame adversity with strength and grace
- Strong test scores
- Managed her ADHD

Veema's Weaknesses

- Freshman and sophomore year grades weak
- Learning difference (but seems under control now)
- Needed to get merit aid, not certain given her rocky beginning of high school

Veema's Checklist

Veema had a bumpy academic record, but it was on the upswing. Since her ADHD was under control and she was more comfortable in her new school, she needed to maintain her higher grades through senior year. She also needed to figure out if she was better suited for the SAT or the ACT with writing and score in the 1800s on the SAT or 27+ on the ACT with writing. This would corroborate her current academic success and show she was ready to succeed at college-level work.

Veema finally found her voice and confidence through her writing and activism. She needed to continue writing short stories and trying to get them published in her school's literary magazine or outside contests. I advised that she should also pursue leadership as president of the Red Cross club or through her involvement in the Gay-Straight Alliance at her high school and Save Darfur rallies. Finally, she needed to take some classes or intern with a photographer to see if that was the route she wanted to pursue in college.

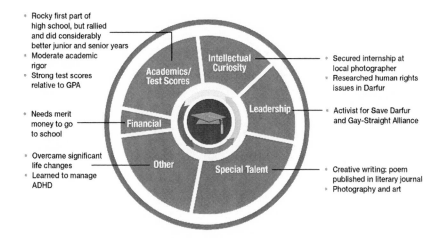

Veema's Application Wheel: Fall of Senior Year

- **Academics:** Veema had a rocky first two years of high school, but she was doing well in her junior year. She needed to continue in this vein throughout senior year to show that her academic progress was consistent.
- **Test scores:** Veema got a 1910 on her SATs and a 27 on her ACTs with writing. She was in good shape for all her schools with these test scores.
- **Athletics:** This was not a part of Veema's wheel.
- **Special talent:** Veema published a couple of short stories in her high school's literary magazine. She was also developing a photo portfolio based on the work she did over the summer.

- **Intellectual curiosity:** Veema showed intellectual curiosity through her internship with a local photographer as well as her interest in Darfur and gay rights.
- **Leadership:** Veema participated in a Save Darfur rally, which empowered her to continue to stand up for what she believed in.
- **Other:** Veema overcame personal hardships with the passing of her grandmother, the marriage of her mom, the birth of her new baby brother, moving, and ADHD. She persevered and as a result became more independent and self-assured.
- **Financial:** Veema needed to get merit aid to bring the cost of a private college on par with that of an in-state school.

Developing the College List

Veema knew that she did best in a small, nurturing environment where she could get to know her professors well and develop a relationship with them. She also enjoyed participating in class discussions and liked direction from her professors. She wanted a liberal arts curriculum that would allow her to explore her many interests, including child psychology, French, and possibly photography, graphic design, and creative writing. She thrived in classes that were more subjective in nature.

Key College Criteria for Veema

- Small to medium liberal arts colleges
- Thought she preferred to be near a city but would have to visit schools to be certain
- A liberal student body with artsy, creative, down-to-earth types who care about humanitarian efforts
- Wanted a moderate workload but needed down time and did not want to be overwhelmed
- Did not care about sports presence or school spirit
- Did not want Greek life to dominate the social scene

- A lot of opportunity to get involved in social action like Red Cross, humanitarian efforts, Gay-Straight Alliance, and so on
- Brand name of the school was somewhat important, but fit was most important
- Opportunity to study abroad
- Overall relationship between price and value would factor highly when determining where she went to college; therefore the fit had to be right

The Final List

We put together a list of schools in all of the categories; however, since merit aid was a key factor in her decision, some of the reach schools were unrealistic. We questioned whether it made sense to even apply to her reach schools knowing that they would be outside of her budget.

The Reaches

- **Skidmore College:** The overall philosophy of Skidmore fit Veema perfectly. They like students with creative combinations. In fact its motto is "Creative thought matters." However, Skidmore is expensive.
- **Sarah Lawrence College:** This school has a very strong liberal arts curriculum, especially in creative majors. There is one-on-one contact with professors and it is an extremely LGBTQ-friendly environment. Cost would be an obstacle.

The Possibles

- **Hobart and William Smith Colleges:** This is a small liberal arts college that is strong in the arts and humanities.
- **Ramapo College:** Ramapo is a smaller public college in her home state, so the price would be right even if she did not get any merit aid.
- **Ursinus College:** This is a great small liberal arts college with strength in her areas of interest.

The Likelies

- **Allegheny College:** The environment was exactly what Veema wanted, and it values creativity. She loved the campus, but it was a little far from home.
- **Eckerd College:** This is a good liberal arts college that offers strong support for students with ADHD.
- **Goucher College:** Veema liked the small, nurturing environment and felt comfortable with the curriculum and student body.

The Safeties

- **Guilford College:** This is a good liberal arts college that with merit aid would fit her budget.
- **SUNY Purchase:** This school has excellent programs in the visual arts and creative writing. Even with out-of-state tuition, it would be within her budget.
- **Susquehanna University:** This is a great small liberal arts college with strength in art and other areas. It has a nurturing environment. One drawback was the rural location.

Choosing an Essay Topic

Veema described herself as hardworking, caring, creative, imaginative, determined, and intellectually curious. She wanted her essay topic to highlight these traits. She felt strongly about social activism and giving back to her community and wanted to make sure that her application essay reflected her passion for these endeavors. As we brainstormed, we recognized several experiences and people that helped her come to this philosophy.

Narrowing Down Possible Topics

Experience: Veema's Major Experiences and Their Impacts

- **Her brother's birth** (made her more caring and maternal). Veema had been an only child living under the undivided attention of her mother and grandmother until she was fifteen years old. It took some time to adjust to not only her baby brother but also her stepfather and her mother's divided attention. At first the changes came as a shock to Veema and she resented them, but eventually she got used to her new family and the changes no longer fazed her. She became bossier and more independent. Prior to her mother's remarriage, Veema had two strong females to depend on (her mom and grandmother), but the marriage, the death of her grandmother, and the arrival of her baby brother actually opened up space for her to become more independent.

- **Summer internship** (became more independent and found her passion). Veema became responsible for herself because she had to research local companies and find an internship. In the past, she would have relied on her mom to do it for her, but since her mom has less time, she could not focus on Veema exclusively anymore. Veema sent out the inquiries, followed up, and eventually landed an internship with a local photographer. She loved working with the photographer and found that she had a knack for interacting with the kids who were sitting for portraits.

- **Moving to a new school** (became more responsible). Veema moved to a new, highly competitive high school at the end of ninth grade. She found the work much harder. She had to step up her game and take responsibility for her own success. If she had trouble, she went to her teachers for extra help. In her old school, the teachers would come to her, but in this new school, she had to take the initiative.

Issue: Personal, Local, National, or International Issue and Its Impact on Veema

- **Darfur** (made her feel more selfless). Veema attended a rally to save the people of Darfur in New York City. She was out there trying to help, and it made her feel powerful, like she could actually do something about it because she was so into it. The energy of the group made her excited and passionate about the cause and provided her with a lot of confidence in her ability to impact change.

Person: Individuals Who Have Had a Significant Impact on Veema's Life and Outlook

- **Mom** (made her focus). Veema said that without her mom she would be all over the place.

- **Cousin** (served as cautionary tale to stay focused in school). Her cousin was a role model for her because he did very well in high school. However, once he went off to college, he started slacking off and ultimately came home. She did not want this to happen to her, so she knew the importance of staying on track in college.

- **Ron Weasley from the Harry Potter novels** (she identified with his initial fear and lack of confidence, but how he ultimately rose to the challenge). Veema adored the Harry Potter books, like most kids of her generation. She saw herself in Ron Weasley; for example, she could relate to getting a howler from her mom if she did not do her work. But on a more serious side, for her summer internship, she initially did not want to apply because it required writing an essay for the application. She thought, "What if I write a bad essay?" She did it anyway and she got in. She was also scared of taking AP French because it would be a lot of work, and she contemplated running away from the challenge, like Ron. Instead she pushed forward and did well. Veema also saw this in her writing. Veema had always loved writing in middle school. When she was in eighth grade she started writing a book. Her cousins read some of it and criticized what she wrote. She left her diary with her cousins and was scared that they would see what she wrote, so she tore out the pages. After that incident, she abandoned her writing until she got to high school. She took a fiction class and wrote numerous slightly morbid short stories. Her teacher entered one of the stories into her school's literary magazine and it was published. After that Veema became more confident in her writing. She feels like writing is more private than speaking, and it provides her an outlet to get her voice out. She likened her experience to Ron's dream of being the Quidditch captain. He couldn't bring himself to try out because he was too scared, like Veema, but eventually he mustered up the courage and succeeded.

■ ■ ■ Possible Essay Topic Summary Chart ■ ■ ■

Experience and Its Impact

Change in family
Provided the space for her to become more independent and learn to embrace change

Internship
Forced her to take initiative and overcome her fear

Moving to a new school
Had to step up her game academically and ask for help

Issue of Importance

Darfur
Empowered her to speak up and become an agent for change

Person and His or Her Impact

Mom
Kept her focused

Cousin
Served as cautionary tale to stay motivated in school

Ron Weasley
Found a character to whom she could relate and who inspired her to face challenges and be confident in her ability to succeed

---

The Personal Statement Essay

Veema decided to write her essay about overcoming the changes in her life through her writing. She wanted to show how she turned to writing as an outlet when she was having a difficult time personally; she felt it was a safe, private place to express herself.

> I grew up in a maternal, overprotective household, pampered by my mother and grandmother. I depended upon them to do things for me so much that they became my voice to the outside world. I yearned to be on stage and recognized, but my timid nature always held me back. I wanted to be social and sometimes perfect, and the only way I could do that was through my own mind. I created worlds for myself where I could recreate past events, but with alternative endings so my voice could stand out. I never wanted to forget the liberating feeling of these perfect worlds, so I wrote them down in diaries along with my stories and poems. Writing was my escape to a "perfect world."

That is, until her family discovered her writing and then she let her fear of their opinion shatter her confidence.

> While visiting my family in Oregon, I tried to write a novel of my own. It was a science-fiction story about a girl and her sister who were abducted by the notorious creature of the lake. Writing this book helped me feel like I was smart, imaginative, creative, and talented. For the first time, I felt confident about myself. Unfortunately, my aunt and cousins had discovered the book while it was still unfinished. My stomach churned, scared of criticism, so I ripped up my book page by page and threw away the shreds. Embarrassed by that incident, I gave up writing for a while.

Veema then described how her family life changed completely over the course of two years and how she turned back to writing to help her cope with the turmoil. But this time, she approached her writing as an adult, not a child.

Over the course of the next two years, my life turned upside down. I moved to a new school, my mother remarried and gave birth to a baby boy, and my grandmother passed away. I could no longer rely on my mother for support since she was equally overwhelmed by all the changes in our lives. Trying to cope with so many changes, I turned back to writing. I joined a semester-long fiction-writing course to help me hone my skills. A few months after the semester ended, my teacher approached me in class and handed me a copy of the school's literary magazine with one of the pages flagged. I opened up to that page and found one of my short stories staring back at me. My heart was pumping with pride and excitement as I listened to my peers and teachers alike praise my work. I enjoyed the liberating feeling of having my own voice out in public and being able to express myself without fear of criticism.

This essay could speak to the Common Application prompt "Discuss an accomplishment or event, formal or informal, that marked your transition from childhood to adulthood within your culture, community, or family" because Veema showed how much she had grown as a writer and as a person. She described her metamorphosis in her conclusion.

For so long, my life trudged along; I felt suffocated in my little safety shell. When I finally cracked open the shell and stepped out, I felt as if I had taken a deep breath of fresh air after being underwater forever. Writing helped me discover kindness in the world and helped me accept criticism instead of hide from it. It helped me embrace who I am, a person who shines most through creativity, expression, and human interaction. I realized how vital all those changes in my life were in order to discover my own voice, and to be my own person. As Eleanor Roosevelt once said, "People grow through experience if they meet life honestly and courageously. This is how character is built."

This experience demonstrated that Veema had the grit and confidence necessary to succeed in college in life. She would no longer run from criticism or change, but instead embrace it.

The Short Answer

Veema was asked to expand on one of her activities in more detail in the short answer. She chose to discuss how empowered she felt when she attended a Save Darfur rally in New York City, because not only did she find her voice for herself, she also found a way to speak for those who had no voice.

> I joined the Help Darfur Now club during my junior year to raise awareness and find a way to stop the genocide in Darfur. I publicized certain events such as movie nights. I also helped recruit people to join our rally in New York outside of Coca-Cola headquarters. During the rally I was thrilled; my blood was rushing madly through my veins. I felt responsible, accomplished, and empowered. I felt like I could make a difference in the world. I obtained the permit for the rally. This year, I've been appointed as one of the officers of the club, and I plan to organize more rallies and activities to raise awareness about the genocide in Darfur. Stopping the genocide in Darfur is important to me, and participating in this club makes me feel like I can play a part to help those who are suffering in the world.

Supplemental Essays by School

Veema had to write two supplemental essays for Allegheny. The first was on "Why Allegheny?" The second described her unusual combination, since that is what Allegheny prides itself on.

Why This School?

Veema wanted a small liberal arts college with a hands-on, nurturing faculty and interesting, creative students that would allow her to explore her many interests. Allegheny fit the bill, so she discussed the academic and social opportunities available and how she just felt the right fit during her visit.

What Are Your Unusual Combinations?

Veema's many interests, ranging from psychology to photography to art to creative writing to French, worked beautifully for this question. She gave some specific ways she would combine her interest in this essay.

Right now I am working on a piece of digital art in Adobe Photoshop using my own pictures. I am attempting to sew together my French and creative writing skills by writing a short story or poem for my school's French magazine, *La Parole*. I have even associated photography with creative writing during my semester-long fiction-writing course. I took a picture of some kind of scenery and I had to write what my teacher called a "setting sketch," where I had to write a story based on the picture, which consisted mostly of describing the scenery. I am looking forward to discovering more ways to find unusual combinations at Allegheny.

Complementary Angles

Letters of Recommendation
- Veema asked her English and French teachers to write letters of recommendation.
- She also got a letter from her boss from her summer internship to speak to her work ethic and creative side.

Brag Sheet/Resume
- Veema emphasized her social action leadership, including her officer position in the Help Darfur Now Club and her involvement in the Red Cross club and the Gay-Straight Alliance. She also highlighted her work and internship experience with a photographer and an ad agency.

Supplemental Materials
- Veema submitted copies of some of her short stories.

Additional Information
- Veema detailed her family information, including the many changes in her life during high school as well as her ADHD and how not taking her medication during the early part of her high school career impacted her grades. She was matter-of-fact and unapologetic, but made it clear that she was in a good place now and had her personal and medical conditions under control.

Interviews
- Veema interviewed at several schools when she visited.

Results

Veema did not apply to any of her reach schools, because she knew she would not get any money. She was accepted (with merit aid at several) to all but one of the schools on her list.

The Possibles
- **Hobart and William Smith Colleges:** Denied
- **Ramapo College:** Accepted
- **Ursinus College:** Accepted

The Likelies
- **Allegheny College:** Accepted ($12,500 per year merit)
- **Eckerd College:** Accepted ($13,500 per year merit)
- **Goucher College:** Accepted

The Safeties
- **Guilford College:** Accepted ($11,000 per year merit)
- **SUNY Purchase:** Accepted
- **Susquehanna University:** Accepted ($15,000 per year merit)

Final Decision

Susquehanna University. Veema was deliberating between SUNY Purchase and Allegheny College. She loved Allegheny but in the end thought it was too far from home. Thankfully, I had visited Susquehanna the week before she had to make her decision and recommended that she at least visit it before deciding, because it had strong liberal arts and a great art program, including graphic design. I also thought she would thrive in the nurturing, family-like community. Sure enough, she visited a few days before May 1 (the final day to matriculate) and decided to attend.

What Can You Learn from Veema's Story?
Questions to Ask Yourself

- Has something in your family or personal life impacted your grades? How so? How did you react to the situation? What can you do to improve the situation?
- Have you abandoned something that gives you pleasure out of fear of criticism or rejection? Can you go back to it?
- Are you too dependent on your family? How can you become more independent?
- Do you have a learning difference that requires medication? Are you taking that medication regularly? Why or why not? How can you get back on track? What else do you need to do to manage your learning difference?
- What are you passionate about? How can you find a way to share that passion with others?
- What can you do to live your life without fear? Can you muster up the courage to move forward? Write down three things you wish you could do and what is preventing you from doing them. Now write down three things that you can do to take the obstacles away.

Notes

CONCLUSION

As you can see from the case studies, everyone has a unique angle.

The ability to identify your unique strengths and effectively communicate them to colleges is the key to admissions success. As you followed the eleven students through their college admissions journeys, hopefully you were able to recognize pieces of yourself that will help you position yourself successfully for college and find your unique angle.

Noah positioned himself through his intellectual curiosity and showed how he discovered the need to listen to multiple perspectives before forming his own opinions. His special talent, acting, provided him a medium throughout high school to get into the minds of multiple characters. At William and Mary, Noah contributed to the community with his open-minded approach to life. He traded his acting for membership in a fraternity and continued to forge relationships with his classmates. He also returned to Panim el Panim (his summer program) as a counselor. As a German studies major, Noah spent a semester studying in Berlin. Upon graduation, he received a Fulbright scholarship to teach English in Vienna, Austria, which led to a Sonnenfeld Fellowship at AJC Berlin, a Jewish advocacy nongovernmental organization.

Feydi thrived at Villanova, taking advantage of every opportunity presented to her. She became a leader in both campus ministry and the Special Olympics. She switched majors from biology to psychology and conducted research in the latter. She maintained her dream to become a physician and pursue a career in medicine, but when applying to medical school, she realized that her leadership skills outranked her science strengths, so she also applied to a master's program in public health. She is currently pursuing a master's in public health and deciding if she will apply to medical school again upon completion.

Kyle successfully transitioned to Muhlenberg and landed a role in the black box theater his freshman year. He followed his path throughout college, mixing his passion for acting with his keen desire to master the business side of the theater and film as well. He graduated and was interning at a talent agency in New York City.

Hayley happily went to University of Texas at Austin, quickly joined a sorority, and found her niche. She found the engineering curriculum incredibly challenging and was contemplating changing majors to something in business. The jury is still out.

Dan jumped right into the UNC Chapel Hill music scene. The professor with whom he developed a relationship during the application stage has served as his mentor for the first year. The college experience is everything Dan had hoped for and more. When we met for coffee over winter break, he mentioned that he was thinking of also adding a business major or minor to his studies, because you never know. (The power of a plan B!) He also landed an internship at Lincoln Center in New York City over the summer because the hiring manager saw his leadership skills and passion for music clear as a bell when they met.

Kaden became a film major at Purchase with a minor in gender studies. He loved the academic side of film and wanted to pursue a PhD in film studies with the intention of teaching film in college. He also remarked how in his gender studies classes, which are predominantly female, his is seen as the stereotypical male point of view. We both chuckled at the irony!

Jenny had a successful year at Ursinus and found the basketball team offered great sense of community to help her make the transition. She loved the small, nurturing academic community and felt right at home.

Adam continued on his science research track and also became very involved in Hillel (the Jewish organization on campus). I met Adam when he was a sophomore for lunch when I toured Johns Hopkins with my daughter. He seemed right at home in the intense academic environment. When we last communicated, he told me that he and his fiancée were headed to Chicago so he could pursue a PhD at the University of Chicago. Once he found his niche among the scientific community, he never wanted to leave.

Francesca thrived at the University of Pennsylvania, but did indeed find the environment challenging. In fact, she told her mom that she had never worked so hard, but she loved the mix of people. Hopefully the next three years will not be so hard!

Hugh heaved a sigh of relief to have the application process behind him. He will spend the summer before he starts Amherst exploring Manhattan and seeing as many shows and celebrity sightings as possible.

Veema graduated from Susquehanna this past May. I spoke with her during her sophomore year when she had some doubts about staying at Susquehanna. We talked about ways to get more involved to find her niche. Upon graduation she had gotten a job working at the school's Center for Diversity and Social Justice, joined the Indian Dance Troupe, and graduated with a degree in graphic design. Once she got back to her roots, she thrived and found like-minded students.

As you can see, each one of these students found his or her unique angle, and so can you. By following the strategies outlined in this book, you can not only survive but thrive during the college application process.

ACKNOWLEDGMENTS

My husband and I spent a few days in the beginning of January recharging at the Lodge at Woodloch in the Pocono Mountains in Pennsylvania. We attended Rhonda Britten's lecture on Fearless Living. She was the guest speaker in residence for the weekend. During her presentation, she asked everyone in the room to identify how fear was keeping them from accomplishing their goals. At first, I remained quiet, but after some other people shared, I raised my hand and said, "I am not sure if it is fear, but I have been wanting to write a book for the past three years and something is holding me back." I scheduled a private coaching session with Rhonda the next day to explore exactly what might be in the way.

We met the next morning, Rhonda still sporting her bathrobe, post–spa treatments. We no longer talked about fear, but instead got down to business and put together a plan to write my book; she also gave me the names of two people who could help me.

I am forever grateful to that weekend at Woodloch and meeting Rhonda, who motivated me to move forward. While writing is a solitary process, Rhonda made me realize that publishing a book requires an army of collaborators and supporters to be successful. Once I got my team in place, I finished the manuscript within six months.

I would like to first thank Martha Guidry, Claire Law, and Steven Antinoff, who served as inspiration to write a book and cheered me on from the beginning. I would also like to thank Doug Crowe for forcing me to move forward on a workbook that preceded the book; Julian Seltzer, one of my students, who worked with me on developing Noah's case study, which served as the template for the rest; and Debbie Pearlson, who wrote the first draft of Jenny's case study.

I am also grateful to my many early readers who provided excellent feedback and encouraged me to keep writing, including Beth Cassie, Diane Forman, Traecy Hobson, Susan Cohen, and Laurie Woog.

I am indebted to my many editors who offered excellent suggestions on the format, content, and case studies, including my daughter, Rebecca Bleich; Richard Lickhalter; Amy Bernhard; Cathy Watts; and Amanda Rooker and her team of editors: Laurel Marshfield, Jessica DuBois, and Lori Paximadis. Lyn Walker and Linda Lyman did an outstanding job of creating the graphics for each student's wheel.

My husband, my biggest cheerleader, has always supported this project, and I thank him for letting me take the risk to write and publish this book. I am also fortunate to have unwavering support from my parents, in-laws, sisters, brother, and daughters.

Finally, I would like to thank my students and their families for the privilege of sharing in their journeys and getting to know them and their unique stories. I feel the joy of their successes and disappointment of their defeats, but I know that every one of them will follow their unique path to becoming their best self. The added benefit of writing this book was the honor of going along for the ride, not once, but twice! I hope that you enjoyed it as much as I did.

ABOUT THE AUTHOR

 Lisa Bleich, founder and president of College Bound Mentor, LLC, is an experienced independent educational consultant, entrepreneur, and writer. She mentors students from all over the world on the college application process, helping them uncover their strengths and develop a personal plan for success. Lisa holds a BA in European cultural studies and French from Brandeis University and an MBA from Harvard Business School. She lives in New Jersey with her husband and three daughters. Two of them have successfully survived the college application process!

CPSIA information can be obtained at www.ICGtesting.com
Printed in the USA
BVOW02s1438180915

418556BV00002B/3/P